Canning Full Circle

From Garden to Jar to Table

Diane Devereaux

canningdiva.com

Written by: Diane Devereaux, The Canning Diva®
Editorial Director: Diane Devereaux
Photography: Jeff Hage, Green Frog Photo
Cover and Book design: Tony Boisvert/Kelsey Kolokowski
Published by: Devereaux Cyber Inc.

ISBN 978-0-9986869-0-5
Printed by: Holland Litho of Zeeland, Michigan

Direct inquiries to The Canning Diva® at www.canningdiva.com

Dedication

To my amazing Mumma who has been my backbone throughout my whole life and my true inspiration in the kitchen,

To my two beautiful children, Caleb and Audrey, for digging in the dirt and canning in the kitchen, for being understanding of my crazy schedule, for appreciating me knowing how hard I work to support their interests and for loving me unconditionally,

To my sister, Deborah for pushing me and supporting me with every hair-brained idea I throw her way,

To Ernie for exposing me to and instilling within me a love and respect for farming, growing and canning,

To Ryan for encouraging me to follow my passion and to my cousin Amy for officially donning me, The Canning Diva,

To my wonderful family, cousins and friends who make my life so much brighter,

To all of my fans who share my passion and love for gardening, canning and preserving,

I want to thank each of you for your unfailing love and support. I dedicate my first printed cookbook to all of you.

My Story

I grew up in inner city Detroit, 6 Mile and Gratiot to be exact. I loved our neighborhood and the fact extended family was nearby making holidays and birthdays fun-filled occasions full of blonde-haired cousins flitting about! Both of my parents and grandparents grew up in Detroit, giving our linage many decades of Motown flair.

When I was 13 we moved to a small town in northern Michigan called Branch. It was a place near and dear to my heart – an annual summer get-away to Grandma Newton's house. Branch had a bar, general store, motel and a Pepsi station. With its one flashing yellow light, I often told people, "if you blink, you'll miss it." What this little town is known for is its acres of forestry, beautiful trails, miles and miles of farmland and the most pristine river, the Pere Marquette.

We lived and worked on a hog farm while our home was being renovated. Here I learned more than a city girl from Detroit ever thought was possible! Thankfully I learned what hard work and reward was truly about. Gardening, tending animals, driving tractor, splitting wood and home canning and preserving. I didn't realize it at the time but Ernie, who I often refer to as my stepdad, taught me valuable life lessons and survival techniques. My mother and he built within me a strong work ethic, integrity, morals and values.

When I finally owned a home of my own the first thing I did was start a garden. My children loved playing in the dirt with me and especially loved harvest time. Since my very first harvest I have been experimenting with canning recipes and often step out-of-the-box making chutneys, creative soups and salsas. One of my signature recipes, Strawberry Salsa (recipe on page 122), landed me on several local news channels where I showcased its simplicity and countless uses.

Today, I am proudly referred to as a valid resource for all things canning and preserving and have donned myself, The Canning Diva®. I have taught over 100 classes throughout West Michigan, created YouTube canning tips, had two radio shows growing listeners to over two million annually and kept working toward my first published cookbook. I am beyond blessed. I am connecting with people on so many levels, sharing what I love most and bringing back this lost art in an era when it's needed most!

Prelude

There is something wholesome and good about home canning and preserving. You know where your food comes from, you take pride and pleasure "putting up" delicious foods for yourself and your family to enjoy during later months – you may even partake in gift-giving and creative mason jar crafts all in the name of Canning. But there is nothing worse than spending all of the time, money and effort of growing, shopping, cutting, chopping, preparing, cooking and processing home canned goods, only to have them go to waste on your pantry shelf.

When I was a new canner, I sought after many recipes that looked cool and exciting. I wasn't afraid to use ingredients I hadn't heard of before. If a friend raved about a new recipe, you better believe I was making a triple batch that weekend. Like many of us, I was just excited to do something good for my family. However, I struggled to find recipes showing me what to make with the home canned goods I had spent hours preserving.

In 2010, I started The Canning Diva® because I wanted to use the knowledge I had about canning, preserving and safe practices to help educate people on this time-honored craft and bridge the generational gap of those who never were taught the art of home canning. In doing so, I revamped family recipes and created new ones I knew my family and friends would love. My focus was to also create recipes demonstrating how to use home-canned goods in practical meal creation.

Teaching people the fun art of water bath canning, demystifying and removing the fear associated with pressure canning and creating fun recipes has been my focus for the last six years now. I am blessed to say that I chose to become The Canning Diva® at the most opportune time given the state of our nation's health, our loose food labeling laws and in an era where growing your own garden or joining a CSA is at its highest since the Great Depression.

While spending the last four years working on my cookbook, I am proud to say I have joined together the best of both worlds – the traditional canning recipe with a meal creation focus. Knowing many of you struggled as I did with traditional canning cookbooks, *Canning Full Circle* was born to encourage growing, preserving and enjoying.

Table of Contents

Chapter 1 - Food Preservation Basics

Chapter 2 - Jams, Jellies & Conserves
To the Jar "Canning"

Chapter 2 - Jams, Jellies & Conserves
To the Table "Eating"

Table of Contents

Chapter 3 - Fruit, Legumes & Vegetables
To the Jar "Canning"

Chapter 3 - Fruit, Legumes & Vegetables
To the Table "Eating"

Chapter 4 - Salsas & Chutneys
To the Jar "Canning"

Table of Contents

Chapter 4 - Salsas & Chutneys

To the Table "Eating"

Chapter 5 - Pickling & Fermentation

To the Jar "Canning"

Chapter 5 - Pickling & Fermentation

To the Table "Eating and Drinking"

Table of Contents

Chapter 6 - Meals in a Jar
To the Jar "Canning"

Chapter 6 - Meals in a Jar
To the Table "Eating"

The Canning DIVA

CHAPTER 1

Food Preservation Basics

Filled with answers to the many questions surrounding food preservation, this chapter will give you an overview of canning and preserving basics including dehydration and dry food storage. Round out your kitchen pantry utilizing the many advantages found in learning the basics.

Food Preservation Basics

I am so excited to share with you my love and passion for home canning and food preservation – and of course cooking! This chapter will break down the basics of how we are able to safely do what we do in our home kitchens, the three main reasons we have the ability to preserve food long-term and various techniques to give you great success when home canning and preserving.

Canning 101

Home canning is such an amazing craft – a lost art that I am having a blast bringing back. There are many misnomers out there scaring people into thinking canning isn't safe. My role is to take the fear out of home canning, teach safe canning practices and create useful recipes families may enjoy making and eating, for years to come!

To start – the best advice I can give to you is, "If you won't eat it, don't can it!"

When my son was a toddler, I got all excited when I found a creative way to flavor applesauce with fresh blueberries. After all, he loved blueberries and loved apples, so putting them together would be even better, right? Looking back, what I should have done was create a small batch FIRST and had him taste it to ensure he liked it. But no, not me. I was all gung-ho and made 22 pints of Blueberry Applesauce (recipe on page 102). I was so proud and excited to open my first jar for him – to incorporate this homemade delight during lunch. Yeah, my beautiful son, Caleb, did not see it that way.

Caleb. Was. Mortified. The horror of two foods being mixed together darn near brought on a meltdown. "Apple swace is not boo, momma" all the while his facial expression were as if I tried feeding him poison. I should have known better. This is the same toddler who detested the mere notion of foods touching each other on his plate. After much coaxing Caleb finally tried a bite…which ended up spat-out back onto the plate. Now, what in the world do I do with 22 pints of blueberry flavored applesauce?

Good news is, through life experience and countless canning endeavors, I created fun recipes so you may utilize your home canned goods to their fullest.

However, if you or your family cannot stand eating peas, no matter how good the sale is, or despite your excitement to pop everything-under-the-sun into a jar (yes, this will happen), resist the urge to can something you know will not get eaten in your home. If you won't eat it, don't can it. P.S. – we eventually ate the blueberry applesauce...because I made muffins...lots of muffins.

A Little History

Many may not know this, but canning as a way of food preservation dates back to the Napoleon War era starting in 1803. In a nutshell, Napoleon was losing the war on the front line because his men were without food – without food his men couldn't sustain. "An army travels on its stomach," Napoleon famously said. By the time fresh foods would make it to the front, they would be rotten and inedible leaving his men to pillage or purchase whatever the native country offered as a food source.

Napoleon put it to his people, through the Society for the Encouragement of Industry, whomever could find a way to preserve large quantities of foods to sustain their soldiers, this person would receive a 12,000 franc reward. Nicholas Appert collected the prize, already knowing that food cooked within a glass jar would not spoil unless exposed to oxygen, hence the need for a good sealing lid. He developed this method of jar sealing not realizing just how necessary it would become.

Fast forward about 50 years and Louis Pasteur discovered how time, temperature and acidic value played a vital role is protecting us from harmful microbes by outlining how to properly process foods. Today, we have a standardized method of safe canning practices of which water bathing and pressure canning play a vital role in giving our households a sustainable food source.

Three Key Players

Throughout my years of teaching canning classes, I begin every class with the basics. Whether you are a veteran canner or a beginner, I make it my job to teach everyone the reasons why we are able to do what we do in our home kitchens. At the forefront are Time, Temperature and Acidic Value.

Let's break it down...

Acidic Value

Food naturally has a pH value. Sometimes that value registers little to no acid; other times it can be highly acidic. On the pH scale, numbers demonstrate the acidic value – the higher the number on the scale, the lower the acidic value whereas the lower the number, the higher the acidic value. For those of you who maintain pools or hot tubs, it is the same pH scale of acid and alkalinity.

When it comes to the acidic value of food, please do not confuse pH acidic value with *flavor*. Let me ask you, what do you think has more acidity; a sweet strawberry or a hot habanero pepper? The answer: a strawberry (3.5 pH) has a higher acidic pH value than a hot habanero pepper (5.8 pH). Spicy or hot *tasting* foods do not mean a higher acidic value on the pH scale.

The reason we must understand a food's acidic value is without the presence of acid, harmful bacteria will grow. Such bacteria will continue to grow in an anaerobic environment, which means a sealed jar in absence of free oxygen. Botulism, a well-known bacteria in canning, can only grow in an anaerobic environment. But did you know potatoes naturally have botulism bacteria on their skin because they grow underground without the presence of free oxygen? Canning doesn't produce botulism. Botulism naturally exists throughout the earth. However, educated canners know how to prevent botulism from inhabiting their food in jars because they understand time, temperature and acidic value and follow tried-and-true recipes.

Another major factor with respect to acidic pH value is to consider the sum of all foods in one recipe, not just the main ingredient. Take, for instance, salsa. Although the main ingredient is tomatoes, which have, on average, a mid-grade level of pH acidity, it is the sum of all ingredients that count most in home canning. Once you start adding onions, jalapenos, cilantro, corn and black beans, you now have diluted, or neutralized, the salsa's overall acidic value. So what do you do when a recipe is lacking acidity? You add acid.

Acid can be in the form of lemon juice, lime juice, vinegar and often wine. When shopping for these products, the key is to ensure the label clearly states a minimum of 5% acidity to be considered safe for home canning. If it is not 5% acidity or higher, do not use it for home canning. Save diluted vinegars for fresh recipes, vinaigrettes or cleaning, and drink the wine…or cook with it!

Time & Temperature

Time and temperature refer to the second stage of canning, which is called processing. The recipe's overall acidic value dictates the proper processing method. There are two processing methods, water bathing and pressure canning. Each method is defined by its temperature output. Water bathing temperature is 212°F while pressure canning is upwards of 250°F. The length of time in which foods process is dictated by the foods acidic value and the temperature required to process.

In my water bath recipes throughout *Canning Full Circle*, you will note not to start the timer until the water is at a full rolling boil. A full rolling boil is the only way to visually ensure the water temperature is at 212°F, the required temperature to kill bacteria in acidic foods. An overall recipe with a high acid content of 4.6 pH or less can be safely water bathed because the temperature in combination with the bacteria killing acid are sufficient for long-term storage.

Foods such as root crops and meat do not have a high acid content, 4.6 pH or higher, so we must rely on time and temperature to safely kill harmful bacteria during processing. Bacteria, yeast and mold grow fastest between temperatures of 40°F and 140°F. When canning low acidic foods, the temperature required to kill harmful bacteria, yeast and mold is 240°F to 250°F. Such high temperatures can only be achieved when using a pressure canner, not a water bather. Pressure canning is the only method of processing that gets food hot enough for long enough, making them safe for long-term storage.

So how will you know which method to use? A tried-and-true recipe will always have the method and the length of time required for processing. If the recipe does not give you this information, get a different recipe from a reliable source. Each of my recipes have been tested in triplicate using a commercial food grade pH tester, stored, then retested to ensure the pH did not deviate. This method of testing is especially important when canning tomatoes and foods that hover around the 4.6 pH mark. For this reason I have often changed the method of processing or added additional acid to the recipe to ensure its safety. A prime example of this is my Basil Diced Tomatoes recipe on page 89. Because it hovered too closely to 4.7pH, it was safest to quickly pressure can this recipe rather than water bath.

Safe Processing Methods

Depending on the elevation, or altitude, of where you live, the rate in which you achieve true temperature when cooking or baking may differ. If you live above 1,000 feet elevation the atmospheric pressure is reduced, causing water to boil at temperatures lower than 212°F. When water bathing, you must increase the processing time to compensate for this difference, and when pressure canning, you must increase the pounds of pressure. Here are two simple charts to help you when processing your recipes in higher elevations.

Water Bathing

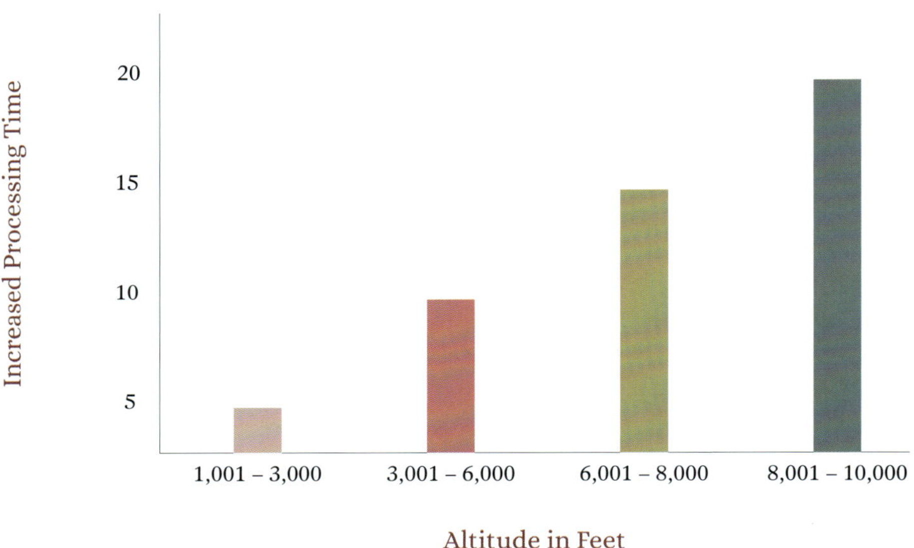

Every canning recipe in *Canning Full Circle* is based on an altitude of less than 1,000 feet, so be sure to adjust according to your elevation.

Water Bathing

Water bathing is the most popular form of processing for many canners. Because the foods processed in a hot water bath are high in acid, such as jams, salsa and pickles, we can rely on the temperature of boiling water. To safely process our recipes, the 212°F water temperature must penetrate the contents of each jar, making it imperative each jar is adequately covered with water. The key is to make sure every jar is covered with at least one inch of water before processing. If processing jars for more than 15 minutes, cover jars with 2 inches of water.

If after processing, any of the jars are exposed to the air (not covered by water), it is likely harmful bacteria will grow in the portion of the exposed food. To remedy this, recover jars with 2 inches of hot water and pre-process for the recipe's specified period of time.

Pressure Canning

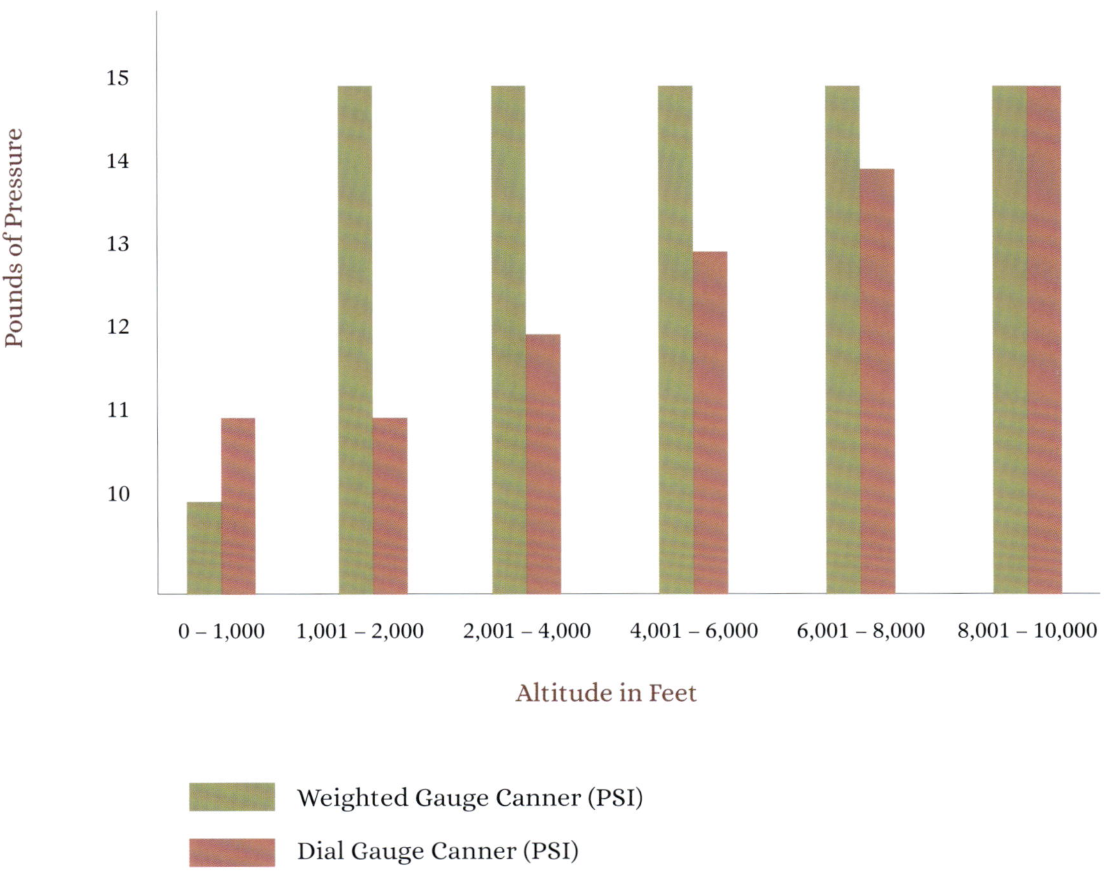

Every canning recipe in *Canning Full Circle* is based on an altitude of less than 1,000 feet, so be sure to adjust according to your elevation.

Pressure Canning

Pressure canning opens the doors to having so many wonderful foods, meals and meats sitting on your pantry shelf! I honestly do not know what I would do without home canned chicken or spaghetti sauce in my pantry. Pressure canning ready-made meals in a jar is not only a time-saver but a much healthier alternative to fast food.

We now know that adding acid to low-acid foods will assist in killing harmful bacteria, but what if adding acid isn't an option because it will ruin the taste of the recipe? I really have no desire to pickle my chicken. To make low acidic foods safe for long-term storage we must rely solely on time and temperature to kill harmful bacteria. In this case, we must exceed boiling water temperatures.

A pressure canner can get upwards of 250°F which is a high temperature attained by air pressure. Unlike water bathing, we are not relying on the temperature of the water to preserve our food in jars, we are relying on the temperature of the air inside the pressure canner. Without the ability to get upwards of 250°F we would not be able to safely preserve soups, stews, chili, meats and many delicious vegetables.

So why can't I just water bath chicken for an extra-long time to avoid purchasing a pressure canner?

I often get this question in my canning classes and lectures. Although I see where your logic is headed, the answer is no, and here is why.

It would take hours to water bath chicken, which may sound feasible until you factor in maintaining a consistent 212°F temperature and factor in evaporation. How will you safely be able to keep the water at a full rolling boil and the jars completely covered with water for hours? Virtually impossible.

Further, there is not a published recipe giving an exact time required to process meat at 212°F, and we all know guessing is extremely unsafe in home canning. Lastly, why risk your health when pressure canners are so readily available for purchase? Is cost preventing you from pressure canning? Keep an eye out at estate sales and thrift stores. A good, used pressure canner with replaceable seals and valves is a great find at a fraction of cost!

Filling & Sealing Jars

There are several key terms often found in canning recipes. Understanding them and properly utilizing their instruction will often be the determining factor as to whether your lids seal or fail. Useful tools such as a headspace measurer and natural bacteria-fighting vinegar are simple, cost-effective ways to substantially decrease lid failures. Properly packing your jars is another key to maximizing yield and utilizing as much jar space as possible.

Raw-Packing Method

This method is most suitable for vegetables and root crops as well as pickling. Raw-packing is the practice of filling jars tightly with fresh, uncooked food. Hence the term, "raw." When using this method it is common to see foods, especially fruit, floating in the jars. The reason foods may float is due to oxygen becoming trapped within the food. Food exposed to oxygen within a sealed jar may oxidize, which means the food may discolor within 3-6 months of storage. It is edible, just discolored. This typically happens to the foods not covered by liquids at the very top of the jar and can happen more often in raw packed jars.

Hot-Packing Method

Hot-packing is the practice of heating freshly prepared food to boiling, simmering for 2 to 5 minutes, then filling jars with the boiled food. Hot-packing is the best way to remove air trapped within food and is the preferred packing method for foods processed in a water bather. Removing trapped air, or pre-shrinking, allows us to better maximize the jar space. Additionally, bringing foods to a boil before packing allows a better flavor transfer, blending ingredients so the overall recipe tastes as it should.

Tip!

Keep your jars looking pristine after processing. Whether water bathing or pressure canning, be sure to add at least one ounce of vinegar to the water. This will keep your jars from being covered in mineral residue found in your water.

Understanding Headspace

The key to lid sealing starts with a clean jar surface and properly measured headspace. Throughout *Canning Full Circle*, you will see my recipes require you to dip a warm washcloth in vinegar and thoroughly wipe the jar rim. Doing so cuts through grease, sugar, brine and removes all food particles atop the jar rim and screw bands, which would otherwise prevent a good seal. Vinegar naturally kills bacteria, so you are giving your jar rim a last line of defense against anything harmful.

It is crucial to proper processing and lid sealing to understand and follow headspace instructions. Headspace is defined as the unfilled space above the food inside a jar and below its lid. Typically in home canning, recipes will specify leaving ¼" headspace for jams and jellies, ½" headspace for fruits, salsa, chutney and tomatoes, and from 1" to 1 ¼" in low acidic foods processed in a pressure canner.

This space is needed for the expansion of food while processing and for forming vacuums in cooled jars. The extent of expansion is determined by the air content in the food and by the processing temperature. Air expands greatly when heated to high temperatures; the higher the temperature, the greater the expansion, therefore greater the headspace. For best results, follow the headspace listed in the recipe.

Over- or under-filling jars also prevents a good lid seal, which is why following proper headspace is crucial to the lid sealing. One of my best examples of this was teaching a canning class where the focal point was pie filling. The class was instructed to work quickly when stirring the pie filling awaiting for it to thicken prior to filling the jars. When bringing the pie filling to a boil, if left unattended, will boil over like an erupting volcano. If the viscosity of the filling acts like this in a stockpot, imagine what it will do in a jar during a hot water bath. To avoid the pie filling from flowing out of the jars during processing, adhering to a 1 ¼", also known as a "generous headspace," will give the pie filling room to expand keeping its contents in the jar.

If you eyeball the headspace and fill it too close to the jar rim, boiling over out into the water bath will cause you to not only lose precious filling, it will spill onto your clean jar rim preventing the lid from sealing.

So how do you measure headspace? At the base of the headspace measuring tool are three notched groves resembling a staircase. Above each notch are embossed measurements from ¼" to 1".

Set the notch measurement specified in your recipe onto the jar rim and hold upright with the tip of the tool placed into the jar. Fill your jar until the food touches the tip of the headspace measuring tool. Be sure the tip is not submerged in food – the tip should just touch the food. If your jar is overfilled, simply use a teaspoon and remove liquid or food pieces as necessary to measure the proper headspace. Once the air bubbles are removed and the headspace is properly measured, you may clean your jar rim in preparation for adhering the lids and rings.

"Remove air bubbles and adjust headspace as necessary." Throughout *Canning Full Circle* you will see this instruction. Removing trapped air is a crucial step in properly packing jars. Headspace measuring tools double as air bubble remover tools. If you do not own one, you may use a chopstick or the handle on a wooden spoon. The key to remove trapped air pockets is using your tool around the inside wall of the jar as well as the center, being sure to tamp down foods to release trapped air. If the recipe has a high liquid content, I will often tamp the jar gently on a cutting board to agitate its contents helping to release trapped air. When canning foods such as raw chicken, it is essential to lift, move and tamp the meat pieces ensuring air pockets cannot form.

Canning with Sugar & Salt

There are so many misnomers out there regarding what is required to home can and what truly does the preserving. Often times I hear it is the salt which does the preserving. For this reason, many refrain from home canning because they heard recipes require more salt than their diet allows. Nothing could be further from the truth. Honestly, controlling what foods go into the jar, including salt, is what makes home canning such a healthy alternative to store bought canned goods.

With the exception of creating brine for pickling recipes, salt is merely for flavor. As described earlier, it is the acidic value of the foods and the processing method that preserves. Take for instance home canned green beans in water. Often recipes state salt in the list of ingredients. Moreover, they state you should include ¼ teaspoon of salt per jar. Anyone with a low-sodium diet knows doing so would be counterproductive, however, many cookbooks fail to tell you salt is optional. Stay healthy knowing salt with the exception of pickling is optional.

This is similar for sugar. A misnomer I often I hear is it's the sugar in jam that preserves the berries or fruit. Well, we now know that isn't the case. What we do know is a plethora of sugar will help with the gelling abilities when exposed to heat, yet many of us cannot ingest 7 cups of sugar for every batch of strawberry jam.

Using Canning Gel to decrease the amount of sugar in jam will increase the berry flavor, lesson the sugar content and increase its thickening ability. It is the only thickening agent approved for home canning as it will not impede heat penetration and retains its viscosity when exposed to high temperatures and acidic foods.

Another beneficial ingredient approved for home canning is Splenda® or low-glycemic Agave sweetener. Keep in mind, when substituting sugar with Splenda® the recipe will have less liquidity whereas adding Agave, the recipe will have more liquidity. Also, both of these options are much sweeter in flavor than traditional sugar.

Thickening Agents

Many canning recipes require a form of thickener whether it is a store-bought powdered pectin, a food starch like Canning Gel or finely chopped apples often used to thicken recipes like chutney.

Pectin, although for the most part derived from natural ingredients such as apple pulp, has limited abilities once exposed to high temperatures for long periods of time. This is often the biggest frustration for first time jam makers. Either their jam never thickens and winds up being used as an ice cream topping or their jam gets scorched from prolonged heat exposure and lack of stirring, which renders the jam useless and inedible.

Another form of pectin is liquid pectin. This clear gel-like pectin is essential when making jelly as the finished product should be translucent in nature. What I have often found when making jelly is the need to double the amount of liquid pectin. Further, the key is timing its insertion perfectly in order for the jelly to set and thicken properly.

Over the years I have perfected what works best with each type of recipe. For instance, the only thickener for pie filling is Canning Gel. Canning Gel is derived from non-GMO corn making it naturally gluten-free. It is corn starch mechanically processed down to a fine powder making it perfect for home canning as it can withstand highly acidic foods and extreme temperatures as well as reheating. Without a food starch such as this you will never achieve gorgeous, gooey pie filling.

Traditional corn starch off the store shelf is not approved for home canning and if used, produces nasty, cement-like looking clumps in home canned goods. Since pectin cannot withstand the prolonged high temperatures it breaks down, causing pie filling to be runny. There will always be a need in my kitchen for liquid pectin; I have simply learned to add more than the recipe calls for to ensure a good gel.

When it comes to thickening recipes in home canning and cooking, I tend to lean toward Canning Gel. I no longer need to purchase powdered pectin, I can reduce the sugar content in my jams, make luscious pie fillings and can thicken pressure canned recipes such as soups, stews, meats and gravies. The best part, I replaced traditional corn starch in my pantry with Canning Gel, since I can use it in everyday cooking, not just canning.

Canning Utensils

We have come so far in technology from when I was a kid it just amazes me! Even something as simple and inexpensive as a magnetic lid grabber makes adding a lid to a jar so much safer. It was always a struggle fighting to get a sterilized lid out of boiling water with only a set of tongs and a pot holder. Remember the days when all we had was a set of tongs to safely empty a sterilized jar full of boiling water while praying it didn't run down our arm? Well thankfully, we've come a long way, baby.

Now while we have made advancements in canning utensils, there are also many useless gadgets on the market. I am sure you've seen them – they look awesome on the infomercial but stay tucked in the back of the utensil drawer for decades. We've all been there. Canning and food preservation is about practicality, so here is a quick list of practical canning essentials that work efficiently and safely:

- **Water bath & pressure canner**
  - There will always be two processing methods to can a variety of foods
  - Some pressure canners can double as a water bather by removing the rubber lid gasket
- **Headspace measuring tool**
  - Ensure proper headspace in jars for a good seal
  - Doubles as an air bubble remover
- **Jar funnel**
  - Save additional work scrubbing jar rims by getting the food in the jar the first time
  - Waste less, can more – maximize jar space
- **Magnetic lid grabber**
  - Get in and out of boiling water safely capturing one lid at a time
  - Avoid touching the underside of the lid, keeping it free from bacteria

- **Racks**
    - Both water bathers and pressure canners require a rack to elevate jars off the heat source
    - A second rack in your tall pressure canner allows you to double stack jars doubling your yield
- **Waterproof, heat resistant canning mitts**
    - Dish towels and pot holders conduct heat when wet, having a waterproof mitt keeps you safe
    - Maintain dexterity when handling boiling-hot, wet jars
- **Large slotted spoon**
    - While many jars can be filled with a ladle, balancing out the ratio of liquids to solids in each jar is essential to best maximize jar space
- **Dishtowels and cutting boards**
    - Keep hot jars off cold surfaces to avoid fracturing the glass
    - Dishtowels soak up water and the cutting boards elevate the jars off countertops
- **Clean, terrycloth washcloths**
    - Reserve a separate washcloth solely for wiping jar rims and screw bands
    - Wiping jar rims with a washcloth dipped in vinegar will remove food debris, kill bacteria and decrease lid failures

These are just a few of the essentials required however there is nothing wrong with expanding upon this list. I love wearing an apron but wouldn't consider it essential. When it comes to safety, I have learned the hard way to protect my hands and face at all costs. For that reason, waterproof heat-resistant canning mitts have become an essential in my canning arsenal.

Long-term Storage

Once your lids have sealed, about 12 hours after removing them from processing, remove the ring and hand wash each jar with soapy water. Dry each jar well and label. I am often asked if the jars should be stored with their rings on. I do believe it is a personal preference, but here is why I store my jars with the rings off.

One winter when my son was 12 years old, I sent him downstairs to our pantry to get two quarts of home canned Chili con Carne (recipe on page 211). As he approached the top of the stairs, one of the lids literally fell to the floor. Obviously this lid came unsealed during storage, which sometimes, but rarely happens. We were able to identify this immediately because the jar was stored with the ring off. The ring was not there to prevent a false impression of a sealed lid. Let's play this scenario out differently…

Let's say I chose to store my home canned goods with the rings on every jar and the lid on that jar of chili became unsealed. My son, being the awesome kid he is, goes downstairs to grab two quarts of chili con carne. Arriving at the top of the stairs it goes unnoticed by him that the lid became unsealed because as far as he can tell it "looks fine." He then takes the initiative to open each jar of chili for me, graciously dumping its contents into the pot to be heated through…and the harmful exposed food goes undetected.

As rare as it might be, I would much rather have my lid come flying off in transit from the basement to the kitchen, or even on the pantry shelf, than it go undetected. So for me in my home, we store with the rings off. Although that was a dramatic scenario, it happened before my own eyes and reassured me of my decision to store with rings off. A less dramatic reason I store with rings off is due to rust. Temperature and humidity fluctuations cause moisture and condensation. Over time, storing with the rings on makes it a blood vessel-popping experience to untwist the ring from the jar and it leaves behind a gross rusty residue on the jar lid and screw bands.

When storing your home canned goods, be sure to store in temperatures between 50°F and 70°F and in an area with limited moisture and sunlight. I will often keep the bulk of my canned goods in my basement and bring one of each up to my kitchen cupboards. Keep in mind, storing these soon-to-use jars in the kitchen is just fine as long as you do not place them in the cupboard above your refrigerator or your stove.

The heat generated from appliances will cause the storage temperature in the cupboard to increase and may also cause condensation in air conditioned rooms.

There are many other places to store home canned goods than in a pantry or kitchen cupboard, especially if space is limited. Try creative areas such as under your bed, in linen closets and in the basement, so long as your home temperature is within the above mentioned range and the area in your home is free from excessive humidity.

Labeling your home canned goods is also essential to eating the most nutritious foods during their prime. When labeling jars for storage include the name of the recipe and the month and year it was processed. Including the month and year on each label is crucial to proper food rotation.

There are two ways to remember how to properly rotate your stored foods: First in, last out. Last in, first out. Foods processed and stored within their first year are at their optimal nutritional value. Within the second year that decreases to roughly 60% and in year three it decreases to 50% or less depending on the food. However, fermented and pickled goods increase in nutritional value when stored properly as they contain probiotics. In a nutshell, eat the older foods first.

Dehydration

In *Canning Full Circle*, we will focus on dehydrating herbs to use in your everyday cooking and canning. And for me, it starts with my garden planning.

I am a huge believer in companion planting to keep pests away. Herbs make excellent companion plants throughout the garden because their aroma deters pests from invading your precious crops. For instance, planting mint, although invasive, will repel aphids, mosquitoes and ants all the while attracting beneficial bees. Planting dill and cilantro will discourage spider mites. The best part, you now have delicious fresh herbs to use when canning, cooking and dehydrating for long-term storage.

Dehydrating is essentially the drying of foods using air current and heat. Home dehydrating foods allows you to dry foods without additives found in many commercially dried goods. The key is removing enough moisture from the foods to prevent spoiling during storage. For this reason it is better to over-dry versus under-dry.

Dehydrated Herbs

Ginger Root

Peel ginger and cut crosswise into thin slices no more than 1/8" thick using a paring knife or course peeler. Place on mesh drying tray. Dry at 130°F for 4 to 4 ½ hours. Store strips intact in a mason jar free from sunlight. Grind into a powder or chop fine before use.

Chives

Remove any tough ends. Place on mesh drying tray. Dry at 130°F for 6 hours. Chives will be very brittle and should break easily when bent. Store in a mason jar free from direct sunlight. Crumble into recipes.

Mint

Remove leaves from stem. Small leaf clusters can be left intact. Place on mesh drying tray with the thickest part of the leaf facing the airflow. Dry at 110°F for upwards of 15 hours. During drying, bring bottom tray up to the top, rotating each tray so it can have an hour or two nearest the heat source and airflow. Store in a stainless steel, airtight container. Keep leaves whole during storage. Steep a dreamy cup of tea with mint leaves or crumble into recipes.

Bay Leaves

Remove leaves from stems and branches. Place on mesh drying tray with the thickest part of the leaf facing the airflow. Dry at 110°F for upwards of 8 hours. During drying, bring bottom tray up to the top, rotating each tray so it can have an hour or two nearest the heat source and airflow. Store whole leaves in a mason jar free from direct sunlight. Use whole leaves in soups and pickling recipes.

Basil

Remove leaves from stem. Small leaf clusters can be left intact. Place on mesh drying tray with the thickest part of the leaf facing the airflow. Dry at 110°F for upwards of 20 hours. During drying, bring bottom tray up to the top, rotating each tray so it can have an hour or two nearest the heat source and airflow. Store whole leaves in a mason jar free from direct sunlight. Use whole or crumble into recipes.

Parsley

Pinch leaf stems with tree segments off the sprigs. Remove any course stems. Place on a mesh drying tray. Dry at 110°F for 8 hours. Leaves should be brittle and stems should break when bent. Store leaf segments whole in a mason jar free from direct sunlight. Crumble or use whole in any recipe or as garnishment.

Cilantro

Remove leaves from stems. Place on a mesh drying tray. Dry at 110°F for 8 to 10 hours. Leaves should be brittle. Store leaves whole in a mason jar free from direct sunlight. Crumble into any recipe.

Sage

Remove leaves from stem. Small leaf clusters can be left intact. Place on mesh drying tray with the thickest part of the leaf facing the airflow. Dry at 110°F for 14 hours. During drying, bring bottom tray up to the top, rotating each tray so it can have an hour or two nearest the heat source and airflow. Store whole leaves in a mason jar free from direct sunlight. Use whole or crumble into recipes.

Rosemary

Do not remove the leaves from the stems. Cut stems off prior to the thick, woody area. Place on mesh drying trays. Dry at 110°F for 12 to 14 hours. During drying, bring bottom tray up to the top, rotating each tray so it can have an hour or two nearest the heat source and airflow. Strip the leaves from the stem and store leaves in a mason jar free from direct sunlight. Use whole or chop fine before use.

Thyme

Do not remove the leaves from the stems. Cut stems off prior to the thick, woody area. Place on mesh drying trays. Dry at 110°F for 12 to 14 hours. During drying, bring bottom tray up to the top, rotating each tray so it can have an hour or two nearest the heat source and airflow. Strip the leaves from the stem and store leaves in a mason jar free from direct sunlight. Use whole or chop fine before use.

Ramp Leaves

After removing bulbs, keep ramp leaves whole. Place on mesh drying try with thickest part of the stem facing the air current. Dry at 110°F for 8 hours. Leaves should be brittle and stems should break when bent. Store leaves whole in a quart mason jar free from direct sunlight. Crumble into any recipe where onion or garlic flavor is welcome. Makes excellent garnishment in place of chives.

Dry food storage

As with any long-term storage plan, keeping your dried goods stored in a dark room without humidity and in temperatures 50°F to 70°F is critical to extending their shelf-life. Mason jars make perfect storage containers for dehydrated herbs and air-tight containers are perfect for dried pantry goods like flour. Neither are fool proof. Here are some tips when storing dried goods for the long haul:

- Store dried goods at least 6 inches off the floor and at least a foot away from any exterior walls – especially if stored in a basement. Temperature and moisture fluctuations are more prevalent when coming in contact with a bare floor and exterior walls. Shelves are a huge asset to prevent such contact.

- When storing flour, add 3 large bay leaves to control moths, weevils, cockroaches, ants and flies. Dehydrating bay leaves and inserting them in dried goods as well as inside your pantry and cupboard shelves is an excellent way to control unwanted pests.

- When storing sugar, add 4 to 6 soda crackers to absorb moisture.

- Food grade, BPA-free plastic 5-gallon buckets with an air tight locking lids are perfect when storing bulk dried beans, rice, flour, powdered milk, salt and sugar.

- Oxygen and moisture absorbers (desiccants) are perfect inside glass, plastic containers and plastic zip seal bags. Four 100cc oxygen absorbers per 1-gallon. Seven or eight 300cc absorbers per 5-gallons. Oxygen absorbers are also sold in 2,000cc and I will often use one per 5-gallon bucket with locking lid. I would suggest two 2,000cc absorbers if your lid does not have a locking mechanism.

- Label everything! Use a black permanent marker where you are able, otherwise make an investment in a label maker. This is very important when storing similar-looking goods such as salt, sugar, flour and powdered milk.

Storing root crops in the winter months

Not everything winds up in a jar in my home. I know it's hard to believe with a title like, The Canning Diva®, but there are many foods I do eat fresh daily. Root crops from my garden fall into this category. My family and I enjoy eating fresh root vegetables and squash all winter long thanks to proper dry storage methods. Here are some tips for storing root crops during the winter months:

- Do not harvest in the rain or on a humid day. The air should be dry for a couple days prior to harvest.
- Do not wash in water, simply brush away as much dirt and debris as possible and cut the tops off close. The exception is beets – cut the stem about 2 inches from the beet.
- Leave your root crops and onions out to dry in the sun light for a full day allowing the exterior skin to thicken and dry out.
- The ideal storage conditions are a temperature range between 33°F and 40°F, humid and no sunlight. This is easily accomplished in homes with basements or in underground storage areas.
- A large wooden box, plastic tote or thick cardboard box is ample space for storing root crops.
- Insulation is crucial to prolonging the life of your root crops. The ideal insulation is peat moss as it self-regulates humidity levels. Saw dust and new, clean play-sand are good options if peat moss is not available. Although I have used unprinted newspaper strips I have found they hold moisture almost too well causing the food to rot sooner.
- Line the box or tote with two inches of insulation and arrange your root crops in the center. They are permitted to touch each other some but not the sides of the box or tote. Be sure there is ample room for air circulation. Cover root crops with a ½" of insulation and repeat until the storage container is full. The top layer of insulation should be about 3" thick. On average a root crop will store well in these conditions for up to 4 months.

CHAPTER 2

Jams, Jellies & Conserves

Take something ordinary and make it extraordinary! This chapter will highlight fun ways to incorporate traditional jams into glazes, desserts and appetizers. I will also highlight how to reduce sugar when making traditional berry jams.

Apple Cider Butter

Makes approx. eight 8-ounce jars or 4 pints

This creamy, smooth spread embodies the flavors of fall! Combining apple cider with cinnamon and cloves, it takes traditional apple butter from ordinary to extraordinary.

Ingredients

6 pounds apples – peeled, cored and chopped (Use your favorite apple)

2 cups apple cider

3 cups raw granulated sugar

1½ teaspoons ground cinnamon

½ teaspoons ground cloves

Instructions

In a large, stainless steel stockpot, add the apple cider. As you are prepping your apples, place them in the cider giving them a quick stir so the cider coats the apples to prevent them from browning. Bring to a boil over medium-high heat, reduce heat and boil gently for 30 minutes. Apples should be soft.

Working in batches, transfer apple mixture to a food processor or food mill and purée. Do not liquefy your apples. Measure 12 cups of apple pureé.

In a thick, wide-bottomed stainless steel stockpot, combine the purée with the spices. Whisk in sugar. Bring to a boil over medium-high heat, stirring frequently to avoid scorching. Once at a boil, reduce heat and boil gently to thicken. Butters may take anywhere from 30 minutes to an hour to properly cook and thicken.

Ladle hot butter into hot jars leaving a ¼" headspace. Remove any air bubbles adjusting headspace if necessary. Wipe rim using a warm washcloth dipped in vinegar, then add lid and ring. Hand tighten. Process jars in a water bath for 10 minutes. Remember, processing time does not begin until water is at a full rolling boil.

Tip!

Have a plate chilling in the refrigerator during recipe prep. Dapple a small amount of apple butter onto the chilled plate. If the butter holds its shape and liquid does not separate from the mixture, your butter is ready to ladle into hot jars.

Apple Cider Butter Muffins

Makes approx. 18 muffins

Break the mold of traditional muffins using your home canned Apple Cider Butter. Its moist texture gives each muffin fluffy softness and gives each muffin an amazing flavor.

Ingredients

1 ¾ cups flour

1 ½ teaspoons baking powder

1 teaspoon baking soda

¼ teaspoon salt

½ cup softened butter

1 cup raw sugar

1 egg

1 cup home canned Apple Cider Butter

1 teaspoon vanilla extract

5 ounces evaporated milk

Instructions

Preheat oven at 350°F. In a small bowl, stir together the flour, baking powder, baking soda and salt. Set aside.

In a large bowl, using a hand beater, beat the butter and sugar until fluffy. Add the egg to the sugar mixture and beat well. Next, beat in the apple cider butter and vanilla. Alternating between the flour mixture and the condensed milk, add one to the apple butter then alternate until all the flour mixture and condensed milk is combined. Do not over mix.

In greased muffin cups, fill each cup ⅔ full of muffin mixture. Bake for 20-25 minutes. Remove from oven and let sit for 5 minutes before placing onto a cooling rack.

Mint Jelly

Makes approx. 4 half-pints

This delicious jelly is an excellent condiment when serving lamb and pork dishes. It is also an excellent way to give a hot cup of tea a minty flavor. Slather your roast with a few Tablespoons of mint jelly to give it a gorgeous sweet mint glaze.

Ingredients

1 ½ cups of firmly packed mint leaves

2 ¼ cups of water

2 Tablespoons lemon juice

3 ½ cups raw sugar

reen food coloring (optional, the mint jelly is tinted with a yellow, green hue otherwise)

1 pouch of liquid pectin

Instructions

Clean and rinse your mint with cold water in a colander being sure to remove any leaves that look ill in appearance. Shake of any excess water and chop finely.

In a large, stainless steel saucepan, combine mint leaves and water. Bring to a boil. Remove from heat, cover and let steep for 10 minutes.

Place cheesecloth over a quart-sized measuring cup and secure with a large rubber band. Gently and slowly pour the mint water over the cheesecloth. Allow the mint leaves to sit and drip until the liquid measures a full 1 ¾ cups.

In a medium, stainless steel stockpot, add mint-flavored water, lemon juice and sugar. Bring to a full rolling boil. Stir in the entire package of liquid pectin – squeezing out every last drop! Boil hard for 1 minute, stirring constantly, being sure to set a timer to avoid scorching the jelly. If you are using green food coloring, add a couple drops and stir. Remove from heat. Skim off any foam from the top of the jelly.

Hot pack into sterilized jelly jars leaving a ¼" of headspace. Using a warm washcloth dipped in vinegar, wipe each jar rim and screw bands. Place sterilized lids and rings on each jar and hand tighten. Process jars in a hot water bath for 10 minutes. Remember processing time doesn't start until the water is at a full rolling boil!

Pan Fried Pork Chops with Mint Jelly

Makes approx. 4 to 6 servings

Mint Jelly is truly an amazing translucent jelly to have on hand for multiple reasons. Often times it is served alongside meat such as pork, chicken and lamb. This is a fun family favorite dinner that is healthy, simple and delicious!

Ingredients

4-6 bone in pork chops

Sea salt and black pepper

3 Tablespoons extra-virgin olive oil

2 Tablespoons real butter

Cayenne pepper – optional

Instructions

The best tasting pork chops truly start with a cast iron skillet. If you do not have a cast iron skillet, don't fret – your pork chops will still be yummy.

Lightly season each side of the pork chop with salt and pepper. If you are adding the cayenne pepper to give your meat a touch of heat, just one dash per side will do. Set aside on a plate.

Using your seasoned cast iron skillet, add the butter and heat on medium-high until butter melts. Add each pork chop and fry for 2 minutes, then flip and fry for an additional 2-3 minutes until the pork chop turns light brown. Now, depending on the thickness of your pork chop, you may need to flip and fry an additional minute or two on each side. The best way to check if your pork chop is done is to either prick the meat with a knife or touch it with tongs or your fingertips. When pricked, if the juices run clear it is done. If touched, it should be slightly firm and spring back to shape after compressing. Otherwise, you may use a meat thermometer in the thickest section of the meat, which should read at least 145°F.

Tip!

Empty a can of Green Beans with Bacon and Cracked Black Pepper into a pan and heat through. In another pan, boil egg noodles with a splash of extra-virgin olive oil and dash of sea salt. When serving the noodles, sprinkle with freshly grated Parmesan cheese, a dash or two of black pepper and a small pad of real butter.

Peach Pistachio Conserve

Makes approx. 6 half-pint jelly jars

I had so much fun creating this recipe! I brought a couple jars to my aunt Maggie's house for taste-testing! Our results: this flavorful conserve is delicious atop goat cheese, complements Foie gras beautifully and makes an excellent addition to a Prosciutto and Pancetta plate. Enhance its flavors by sprinkling a touch of Himalayan sea salt prior to serving!

Ingredients

2 cups unsalted, shelled Pistachio nuts, chopped

4 cups peaches, peeled and finely chopped (approx. 8 peaches)

2 cups sweet cherries, pitted and coarsely chopped

Zest and juice from 2 large oranges

2 cups golden raisins

1 Tablespoon fresh gingerroot, grated

¼ cup fresh mint, finely chopped

2 Tablespoons lemon juice

6 Tablespoons Canning Gel

Instructions

Pistachio Prep: In the event you cannot procure unsalted nuts, place salted pistachios in a colander in the sink and rinse thoroughly until the salt has been removed. Simply pat pistachios dry before chopping.

In a large, stainless steel stockpot, combine all ingredients, less the Canning Gel, and bring to a boil over medium-high heat. Stir constantly to avoid scorching. Once at a boil, reduce heat and whisk in Canning Gel. Boil gently for 10 minutes, stirring frequently to avoid scorching as the conserve thickens.

Ladle hot conserve into hot jelly jars leaving a ¼" headspace. Remove any air bubbles and adjust headspace as necessary. Using a warm washcloth dipped in vinegar, wipe jar rims and screw bands. Add sterilized lids and rings and hand tighten.

Place jars in a water bather and cover with 1 inch of water. Process jars for 15 minutes. Remember, processing time does not begin until the water is at a full rolling boil.

Charcuterie Plate

Approx. 4 to 6 servings

This crowd-pleasing hors d'oeuvres can often be seen at high-end restaurants, but now you can enjoy it in your own home with just a few, fun tips from The Canning Diva®.

Your home canned Peach Pistachio Conserve will wow your guests and become a wonderful introduction to any meal. Personally, I love munching on this scrumptious app while sipping a Basil Hayden Whiskey on the rocks with an orange slice – the perfect array of flavors dance across your palette.

Charcuterie Plate

Ingredients

Meats – The real fun begins with a variety of cured and thinly sliced cuts. Here are some options to choose from – depending on your guest list, be sure to purchase at least 2-3 ounces per person when shopping.

Sausages – smoked chorizo or saucisson sec are popular favorites along with a cooked garlic sausage

Paper-thin Muscle Cuts – a cured pork tenderloin like lomo or cured beef tenderloin like bresaola

Smoked Country Hams – Prosciutto offers many varieties like Jambon de Bayonne, a French prosciutto or something fun like duck or boar prosciutto

When in doubt, ask your butcher.

1 pint jar of Peach Pistachio Conserve

1 pint jar of Pickled Garlic Cloves – optional

½ cup blonde raisins

2 Tablespoons raw honey

1 medium size gingerroot

6-8 ounces Brie cheese

Himalayan sea salt

1 baguette cut into 1" thick slices or 1 box of peppered rice crackers

Instructions

Now this is the fun part! Grab your favorite serving platter or use a large wooden cutting board. Taking each slice of meat, lightly fold and drape across each other into a decorative pile, keeping the various meats grouped accordingly. Peel the exterior of the ginger root to unveil the fresh center. In long, firm strokes, peel enough zesty strips so your guests have at least two each.

Fill a ½ cup container, the sassier-looking the better, with your Peach Pistachio Conserve and another with your Pickled Garlic Cloves (recipe found on page 181). Feel free to create a cute pile of raisins off to one side, smear the honey off into one corner, place the ginger strips in another, and cut the Brie into ¼" thick slices and pile alongside the sliced baguette. There's no wrong way to create a Charcuterie Plate – so have some fun with it!

Jalapeño Jelly

Makes approx. 8 half-pints or 4 pints

Yes, you read it right – jelly made from jalapeños. Not to worry! This delightfully sweet jelly has just a touch of heat and is full of flavor! This versatile jelly makes an excellent gift during the holiday season.

Ingredients

1 cup jalapeño peppers, puréed or chopped extra fine

¾ cup Bell pepper – I like to use yellow and red bell peppers for contrasting colors

1 ½ cups white vinegar

2 6oz packages of liquid pectin

6 ¼ cups sugar (If you use raw sugar, the color of your jelly will be a bit darker; white granulated will give a more translucent hue)

Instructions

Jar Prep: Because this recipe requires water bathing for 10 minutes, it is important to sterilize your jars prior to filling them. Once sterilized, have them set in boiled water. Sterilizing your jars prior to processing gives them a "leg up" when killing bacteria during processing.

Finely chop jalapeños and bell peppers in a food processor. The best way to gauge the speed at which you achieve this texture is by "pulsing" the food processor. Do not liquefy the peppers.

Mix peppers, sugar and vinegar in a stainless steel stockpot. Bring to a rapid boil on medium-high heat for 3 minutes – be careful not to scorch! Add the liquid fruit pectin, mix well and boil for 1 minute. Be sure to set a timer – guessing (or counting) never works!

Remove from heat and let stand for 5 minutes to thicken. Ladle into hot, sterilized jars being sure to leave a ½" headspace. Remove any air bubbles and adjust headspace if necessary. Wipe rim and screw bands with warm washcloth dipped in vinegar. Place sterilized lid and rings onto jars and hand tighten.

Process in a water bath; 10 minutes for half-pint and 15 minutes for pints. Remember, processing time does not begin until water is at a full rolling boil!

Creamy Jalapeño Jelly Appetizer

Makes approx. 6 to 8 servings

Although this appetizer is a simple one, it is a pleasing one. The delectable flavors of the sweetened jalapeños match perfectly with the creamy cheese and salty cracker. This is a go-to app when company arrives or I am invited to a BBQ with friends. Attending an event with more than 8 people? Simply double this recipe for twice the enjoyment.

Ingredients

1 pint jar of Jalapeño Jelly

1 brick of cream cheese

1 box of salted crackers

Instructions

Keeping the cream cheese in its wrapper, place the brick on the counter top for a half hour to soften. Once soft to the touch, remove the cream cheese from its wrapper and place in the center of a large plate.

Cover the entire brick of cream cheese, being sure to pile it high. Using a butter knife, move the jelly about so it lightly covers the sides of the brink, allowing some to fall onto the plate covering the brink completely.

Line a basket with a linen cloth and empty the box of crackers into the center. Place two small appetizer knives alongside the jelly covered cream cheese and serve.

Braised Red Cabbage

Makes approx. 6 servings

A seasonal favorite in my home around Thanksgiving and Christmas. Braised Red Cabbage is a colorful addition to any spread no matter the occasion. Add a kick of flavor to this traditional favorite with your home canned Jalapeño Jelly! The sweet heat of the jelly balances out the tart flavors of the vinegar and cabbage.

Ingredients

4 Tablespoons butter

1 Tablespoons raw sugar

1 teaspoon sea salt

⅓ cup water

⅓ cup white vinegar

¼ cup home canned Jalapeño Jelly

1 small head red cabbage, cored and thinly shredded

½ cup apple, peeled and coarsely grated

Instructions

Preheat oven to 350°F. Combine butter, sugar, salt, water, vinegar and jelly in deep saucepan over medium heat. Bring mixture to a boil stirring until all has dissolved. Add shredded cabbage and grated apple and mix to coat. Transfer to a large baking dish with lid.

Cover and bake for 1 hour. Remove lid and stir. Bake for an additional hour. Remove from oven.

Allow to sit for 5 minutes with the lid off. Mix before serving to ensure any liquid that settled to the bottom of the dish coats the cabbage.

DIVA
Canning
Gel

Less Sugar Berry Jam

Makes approx. 5 half-pint jars

There is something to be said about having a delicious, homemade berry jam on your pantry shelf! Some say once they have experienced a homemade jam they rarely, if ever, purchase store bought jam again. Many on the other hand say they would love to make and eat homemade jam but cannot ingest the amount of sugar called for in standard recipes. By using Canning Gel as a natural thickener, we can drastically decrease the sugar content without losing the jam's gelling abilities, and keep the berry flavor.

Ingredients

4 cups berries, crushed (any berry of your choice)

¼ cup lemon juice

7 Tablespoons Canning Gel

1 ½ to 2 cups raw sugar, to taste

Instructions

Using a colander, clean your berries being sure to remove any stems and suspect berries. In a medium sized bowl, working in batches, use a potato masher and crush the berries. Measure crushed berries and some of their juice. Continue this process until a full 4 cups is achieved. This recipe can be made successfully in triplicate.

Place crushed berries in a thick bottom, stainless steel stockpot. Add lemon juice and stir.

Stir the Canning Gel into ¼ cup of the sugar. Add sugar mixture to the berries. Bring contents to a boil using medium-high heat and stir constantly. Add remaining sugar. Bring back to a boil. Set timer and boil for 1 minute. Remove from heat.

Ladle hot jam into hot sterilized jars leaving a ¼" of headspace. Remove air bubbles and adjust headspace as necessary. Using a warm washcloth dipped in vinegar, wipe jar rims and screw bands. Place sterilized lids and rings atop each jar and hand tighten. The jam will be lighter in color prior to processing. After processing, it will be a vibrant color mirroring the berries used to create your jam!

Place jars in rack inside the water bather being sure jars are submerged and covered with an inch of water. Process jars half-pints for 10 minutes, pints for 15 minutes. Remember, processing time doesn't begin until water is at a full rolling boil.

Blackberry Peach Jam

Makes approx. 5 to 6 half-pint jars

You will be amazed by this combination of fruits! Using the less sugar jam premise, this delicious jam boasts unbelievable flavors that will jump-start your taste buds. The sweet tones from the peach balance-out the tartness of the blackberries. Perfect for a PB&J sandwich or in the center of a cupcake – the uses are limitless.

Ingredients

4 cups crushed blackberries

1 large peach, pitted and peeled

¼ cup lemon juice

7 Tablespoons Canning Gel

1 to 1 ½ cups raw sugar

Instructions

Using a colander, clean your berries being sure to remove any stems and suspect berries. In a medium sized bowl, working in batches, use a potato masher and crush the berries. Measure crushed berries and some of their juice. Continue this process until a full 4 cups is achieved. Next, chop the peeled peach into small chunks then crush using a potato masher.

Place crushed berries in a thick-bottomed, stainless steel stockpot. Add lemon juice and stir. Measure ¼ cup of the sugar and stir in all 7 Tablespoons of Canning Gel. Add sugar mixture to the berries and whisk well. Bring contents to a boil using medium-high heat, stirring constantly. Add remaining sugar. Bring back to a boil. Set timer and boil for 1 minute. Remove from heat.

Ladle hot jam into hot sterilized jars leaving a ¼" of headspace. Remove air bubbles and adjust headspace as necessary. Using a warm washcloth dipped in vinegar, wipe jar rims and screw bands. Place sterilized lids and rings atop each jar and hand tighten.

Place jars in rack inside the water bather being sure jars are submerged and covered with an inch of water. Process jars for 10 minutes. Remember, processing time doesn't begin until water is at a full rolling boil.

Blueberry Lime Jam

Makes approx. 7 to 8 half-pints

The most versatile of all jams! Best part, it zings with flavor – a fun twist on a traditional favorite. Use it on sandwiches but have fun glazing meats or creating delicious desserts.

To the Jar

Ingredients

4 ½ cups blueberries, crushed (Will need about 9 to 10 cups of whole berries to achieve this)

1 large lime, all its juice and grated zest

7 Tablespoons of Canning Gel

5 cups sugar, raw or unbleached – granulated

Instructions

Rinse blueberries in a colander. Shake off extra water before spilling the clean berries onto a cookie sheet. Using your hands, sift through the berries being sure to remove stems and any damaged, spoiled, unripe or mushed berries.

Using a large measuring bowl add one cup of berries at a time and mash with a potato masher. Mash berries until you no longer see any whole berries left. Continue to add additional berries until you measure 4 ½ cups.

Placed mashed berries into a stainless steel stockpot. Combine berries, lime zest and juice, mix well. Stir sugar and Canning Gel together in a bowl. Add to berries and mix well.

Bring to a boil while stirring constantly. Skim off any foam. Using your funnel and a ladle, fill sterilized half-pint jars with hot jam leaving a 1/4" headspace. Wipe the rim and screw band with a warm washcloth dipped in vinegar prior to adding the prepared lids and rings. Hand tighten. Process in a hot water bath, 10 minutes for half-pint, 15 minutes for pints. Remember, processing time does not begin until the water is at a full rolling boil.

Tip!

Set a timer! It is amazing how quickly our jam can be ruined from scorching simply because we thought it'd be easier to "count to 60."

Blueberry Crumble Bars

These delicate crumble bars are the perfect complement to a morning cup of coffee and can make for a light dessert after dinner. The beautiful blend of blueberries and lime baked inside each bar is one of my favorite uses for this zippy jam.

Ingredients

1 cup raw sugar

1 teaspoon baking powder

3 cups flour

1 cup cold unsalted butter

1 egg

¼ teaspoons sea salt

1 pint Blueberry Lime Jam

Instructions

Preheat oven to 375°F. Grease a 9x13 baking dish and set aside.

In a bowl mix sugar, baking powder, salt and flour. Using a hand beater on low, fold the butter into the flour mixture. Add the egg and beat well until the mixture looks like small peas. Split the mixture in half. Pat one half into the greased baking pan. Set the other half aside.

Using a rubber spatula, spread your Blueberry Lime Jam into a ¼" to ½" thick layer atop the dough inside the pan. Crumble remaining dough evenly atop the jam.

Bake for 45 minutes or until top is slightly brown. Cool completely before cutting and removing. When cooled, cut into 3" bars and store in refrigerator. Serve with fresh blueberries and lime zest.

CHAPTER 3

Fruit, Legumes & Vegetables

This chapter is chock-full of amazing recipes, so you can enjoy fresh fruits and vegetables year 'round. Make amazing side dishes, delicious pies, hearty soups and casseroles with your home canned fruit, vegetables and beans.

Pressure Canning Pumpkin & Squash

To the Jar

Fall is the season for pumpkins, squash and gourds – and all things harvest fun! Although these vegetables last for months in dry storage, preserving their freshness in a jar will ensure you enjoy them well into spring and summer!

You will need about 2 ½ pounds of pumpkin/squash for every one quart jar. If canning in pints, 2 ½ pounds will yield approximately two pint jars. Because the interior flesh of pumpkin/squash is so dense, especially when mashed or puréed, it is not recommended this vegetable be home canned in such a dense state. It is best to cube or dice large then pressure can.

Instructions

Wash the exterior of your squash being sure to remove any dirt or debris. Cut squash in half and remove all of the seeds using a large spoon. Using a peeler, carefully remove the rind. Cut the flesh into 1" cubes.

In a large, stainless steel stockpot, cover cubed squash with boiling water. Bring to a boil over medium high heat and boil hard for 2 minutes. Fill a second stockpot of water, bring to boil.

Drain cubes in a large colander. Using a ladle and funnel, pack hot cubes into hot jars being sure to leave a generous 1" headspace.

Ladle fresh boiling water over top of the cubes, keeping the generous 1" headspace. Use your air bubble remover tool to remove any excess air. Adjust headspace if necessary.

Wipe jar rims with a warm washcloth dipped in vinegar. Place prepared lids and rings on each jar and hand tighten. Process in a pressure canner at 10 pounds of pressure; pints for 55 minutes and quarts for 90 minutes.

Ball
sealed for freshness
Made in USA

Green Beans with Bacon

Makes approx. 9 quarts or 18 pints

As a mom with two kiddos I know I must keep meals interesting and tasty, especially if I want them to eat their green vegetables! So what do I do...I add bacon! And we all know everything's better with bacon! This recipe makes a delicious side dish and a great Green Bean Casserole starter for holiday dinners. If you are on a low sodium diet or do not eat pork, feel free to not add bacon – the green beans are just as tasty all on their own!

Ingredients

10 pounds of green beans

2 pounds of thick cut bacon

Fresh cracked black pepper

Instructions

In a large skillet, fry up bacon slices until crispy but not burnt. Cool bacon in paper towel to remove excess grease. When bacon has cooled, crumble into small pieces OR tear into 2" strips and set aside in a clean bowl.

Using a colander, wash the beans under cold running water. Disregard any ill-looking and rusty beans. Remove stems and leave the end tip. Cut beans in bite size pieces approximately 2" in length. Place prepped beans in a stockpot and cover with water. Bring green beans to a boil over medium heat. Allow to boil for 5 minutes, stirring a few times to evenly distribute the heat.

Using hot, clean jars add 1 Tablespoon/two 2" pieces of bacon and 1/8 teaspoon black pepper to each pint jar and 2 Tablespoons/four 2" pieces of bacon and 1/4 teaspoon black pepper to each quart jar. Using a slotted spoon, fill your jar with green beans being sure to leave a 1" headspace. Ladle hot bean liquid over top of the beans keeping the 1" headspace. Remove any air bubbles and readjust headspace if necessary.

Wipe each rim with a warm washcloth dipped in vinegar. Add lids and rings then hand tighten. Place jars in pressure canner and process at 10 pounds of pressure; quarts for 25 minutes and pints for 20 minutes.

Ball

Green Bean Side Dish

Makes approx. 9 quarts or 18 pints

Green beans with bacon make an excellent side dish straight from the jar. Simply heat through and enjoy its excellent source of nutrients and flavor – the perfect addition to any meal.

Green Bean Casserole

Makes approx. 6 servings

Like many, we love adding this traditional dish to our table around the holidays. Use your delicious home canned Green Beans with Bacon for a fun twist in flavor and a side dish sure to please.

Ingredients

1 cans condensed cream of mushroom soup

½ cup whole milk

1 Tablespoon soy sauce

½ teaspoon black pepper

½ cup fresh bean sprouts

2 quarts home canned Green Beans with Bacon, drained

2 cups French fried onions

Instructions

Preheat oven to 350°F.

In an oven-safe 2 quart casserole dish, mix soup, milk, soy sauce, bean sprouts, drained green beans with bacon and ½ cup of onions together to ensure beans are thoroughly coated.

Bake for 25 minutes or until it bubbles. Carefully stir ingredients well and top with remaining French fried onions. Return to oven for an additional 5 minutes to lightly brown the onions. Serve hot.

Tip!

Want more bacon flavor? Fry 5 strips of bacon while casserole is baking. Crumble cooled bacon atop the remaining French fried onions prior to returning to oven for browning.

Ball

Beets in Water

Makes approx. 4 quarts or 8 pints

There are many benefits to home canning beets. You may use them as a side dish to accompany any meal, slice them for salads and even sandwich toppers.

Ingredients

12 pounds fresh whole beets – with stems and roots on

Instructions

You will need two stockpots. One to boil beets and one of boiling water to hot pack.

Beet Prep: Cut stems leaving 2" and keep the root. Blanch for 30 minutes in boiling water. Cool in bowl of cold water in the sink. Under cold stream of water, use thumbs and slide skin off beat. On cutting board, remove stem and root. Quarter large beets and leave smaller beets whole – be sure to keep beets uniform in size.

Bring prepped beets to a boil. Boil for 5 minutes then hot pack into jars being sure to keep a 1" headspace. Using your funnel, ladle fresh boiling water over the beets, keeping the 1" in headspace.

Remove air bubbles and adjust the headspace as necessary. Wipe jar rims and screw bands using a warm washcloth dipped in vinegar. Place lid and rings on and hand tighten. Process in a pressure canner at 10 pounds of pressure; 30 minutes for pints and 35 minutes for quarts.

Tip!

It is important in home canning to keep vegetables uniform in size. This allows the required temperature during processing to adequately penetrate the foods.

Beet Salad

Makes approx. 4 servings

Beet salad is a family tradition that is a nostalgic delight shared by many of my cousins. This simplistic salad is power-packed with nutrients and is a gorgeous presentation. Serve cold alongside any meal – or if you're like me – a salad makes a fantastic lunch.

Ingredients

1 quart home canned beets

1 cucumber, peeled and chopped

5-6 ounces goat cheese

Chives, chopped fine (optional)

Instructions

In a large, stainless steel bowl, crumble the goat cheese. Drain a quart of beets and chop beets into bite-size pieces. Add chopped beets and cucumbers to the goat cheese and mix well.

Cover bowl with plastic wrap and place in refrigerator for 30 minutes.

Remove from refrigerator and mix again. Place chilled salad into a serving bowl and garnish with chives before serving.

Borscht aka Beet Soup

Makes approx. 6 to 7 quarts

If you like beets, you'll love Borscht! This fun spin on a Russian variety is a hearty meal even finicky eaters will enjoy. Serve hot and add a touch of sour cream and garnish with a fresh sage.

Ingredients

3 Tablespoons extra virgin olive oil
2 medium onions, chopped
½ head cabbage, sliced thin
2 carrots, shredded
2 Roma tomatoes, diced
12 garlic cloves, chopped
24 medium beets, chopped
2 cups Cabernet Sauvignon wine
8 cups beef stock
1 Tablespoon raw sugar
1 Tablespoon sea salt
1 teaspoon black pepper

Instructions

Beet Prep: Cut stems leaving 2" and keep the root. Blanch for 30 minutes in boiling water. Cool in bowl of cold water in the sink. Under cold stream of water, use thumbs and slide skin off beat. On cutting board, remove stem and root.

Chop skinned beets into 2" pieces and set aside. In a stainless steel stockpot, add olive oil and sauté onions, garlic, carrots, cabbage and tomatoes until the onions become translucent. Sauté About 8 minutes. Add the beef stock and bring to a boil. Stir in chopped beets and allow to boil for an additional 2 minutes. Remove from heat.

Once cool enough to handle, working in batches, place the beet mixture in the food processor and pulse until it is a fine puréed texture. Once all of the beet mixture is puréed, return to a clean stainless steel stockpot. Add the red wine, sugar, salt and pepper. Mix well.

Using medium heat and stirring frequently, allow the borscht to gently heat through, about 5 minutes. Be careful not scorch the borscht!

Remove from heat and ladle hot soup into hot quart jars, leaving a 1" headspace. Using a warm washcloth dipped in vinegar, wipe the rim of each jar before placing the lid and ring on top. Hand tighten.

Place quart jars in pressure canner and process at 10 pounds of pressure for 90 minutes. If using pints, process at 10 pounds of pressure for 75 minutes.

Enjoying Borscht

This hearty, fuchsia soup can be served hot or cold! When served hot, it is the perfect soup on a cold winter day or if your immune system needs a boost. In the summer, chilled Borscht it is a delightful alternative to gazpacho.

Served Hot

Empty a quart of Borscht into a saucepan and bring to a boil over medium heat, stirring often. Garnish and serve alongside buttered biscuits or beer bread.

Served Cold

In a large bowl, mix 1 quart of Borscht with ½ cup of kefir or plain Greek yogurt. Cover and place in refrigerator to chill for at least 4 hours or overnight. When ready to eat, stir well then place in bowls, garnish and serve.

Garnish Ideas

A dapple of sour cream with a fresh sage leaf or two is common. If you prefer basil over sage feel free to do so. If you would like to pull the garlic and onion flavors from the soup, sprinkle chopped chives overtop. Fresh dill and parsley are also great ideas depending on your flavor palate.

Sweet Potatoes

There are many fun reasons to have this healthy potato on the ready. It makes an excellent side dish and an even better sweet potato pie. Although I talk in "pounds" in the recipe, I suggest having at least 15 large potatoes on hand to make pressure canning this delicious root crop worth the time investment.

Ingredients

You will need about 2 ½ pounds of sweet potatoes for every one quart jar. If canning in pints, 2 ½ pounds will yield approximately two pint jars.

Like pumpkin/squash, the sweet potato is dense when mashed or puréed, so it is best to quarter or cube keeping the pieces as uniform in size as possible. When it is time to use your home canned sweet potatoes, you may drain them then mash or purée depending on how they are being used in a recipe.

Instructions

Wash the exterior of your sweet potatoes being sure to remove any dirt or debris. Using a paring knife, make a slit around the entire middle of the potato, gently scoring the skin. In a large, stainless steel stockpot, add your scored potatoes and cover with warm water. Bring to a rapid boil on high heat, boiling the potatoes for 20 minutes.

Remove potatoes and place on cutting board to cool until safe to touch. Remove skins and either quarter or cube. While potatoes are cooling, bring a stockpot full of fresh water to a boil.

Hot pack potatoes into pints or quarts leaving a 1" headspace. Ladle fresh boiling water over potatoes being sure to keep the 1" headspace. Remove air bubbles and adjust headspace as necessary.

Wipe jar rims with a warm washcloth dipped in vinegar. Place prepared lids and rings on each jar and hand tighten. Pressure can at 10 pounds of pressure; pints for 65 minutes and quarts for 90 minutes.

300
200

Sweet Potato Pie

A fall favorite in our home especially around the holidays! Save yourself the potato prep by putting your jars of pressure canned sweet potatoes to good use. A traditional pie requires 2 cups mashed sweet potatoes, which requires about 1 quart canned cubed sweet potatoes.

Ingredients

1/3 cup butter

3/4 cup light brown sugar

2 eggs, lightly beaten

3/4 cup evaporated milk

2 cups mashed sweet potatoes

1 teaspoon vanilla extract

1/2 teaspoon ground cinnamon

1/2 teaspoon ground nutmeg

1/4 teaspoon ground allspice

1/4 teaspoon salt

Mumma Newton's Pie Dough (page 110)

Instructions

Preheat oven to 400°F. Place pie dough in a 9" baking dish. If using store-bought dough, lightly brush with melted butter. Bake crust for no more than 10 minutes to set the dough. Remove from oven and reduce oven temperature to 350°F.

Drain one quart, or two pints, of home canned sweet potatoes in a colander in the sink. Let set to drain.

In a mixing bowl, blend together the butter and sugar using a handheld electric mixer until it forms a creamed consistency. Be sure to use a rubber spatula to pull sugar and butter off the wall of the bowl and back to the center.

Remove sweet potatoes from colander and place into a large measuring bowl. Mash with a hand masher and measure 2 cups.

Add beaten eggs and blend again, pulling mixture from the sides of the bowl. Add evaporated milk, drained sweet potatoes, vanilla and spices. Blend well using the same technique.

Pour mixture into pie crust being sure to smooth out the top with spatula. Bake until for about 1 hour or until a knife inserted in the center comes out clean. Cool completely on wire rack before serving.

Creamed Sweet Potatoes & Sage

Makes approx. eight 4-ounce servings

I love making this during Thanksgiving as a festive and delicious side dish. Best part, it is another way to use for your dehydrated herbs and home canned goods. This recipe will yield about 4 cups mashed Sweet Potatoes & Cream.

Ingredients

2 quarts pressure canned sweet potatoes

3 Tablespoons butter, softened

2 Tablespoons dehydrated sage

¾ cup evaporated milk

Sea salt and black pepper, to taste

Instructions

Preheat oven to 375°F. Drain home canned sweet potatoes in a colander in the sink. Remove sweet potatoes from colander and place into a large mixing bowl. Add butter, milk and dehydrated sage to potatoes. Add a dash or two of salt and pepper.

Using a hand-held electric mixture, blend ingredients until it forms a creamed consistency. Be sure to use a rubber spatula to pull foods off the wall of the bowl and back to the center. Once blended, increase speed and whip for 1 minute.

Transfer mixture to a 2-quart casserole dish. Crush several dehydrated sage leaves in the palm of your hand and sprinkle atop of the sweet potatoes. Cover and bake for 40 minutes.

Tip!

Use your dehydrated sage leaves to garnish prior to serving. Crumble or leave whole – either makes an excellent presentation.

Basil Diced Tomatoes

Makes approx. 8 pints or 4 quarts

Need an alternative to stewed tomatoes? Give my Basil Diced Tomatoes a try. Slices of garlic, fresh basil leaves and a touch of black pepper make these the most versatile tomato in your pantry.

I use Basil Diced Tomatoes in soups, stews or over baked chicken. Sometimes I'll just heat up a jar and toss with pasta if I'm not in the mood for a heavy sauce. The possibilities are endless!

Ingredients

16 cups of cored, diced Roma tomatoes – I leave the skins on

1 large yellow (or green) bell pepper, chopped

1 large onion, chopped

2 Tablespoons of fresh garlic, minced

¼ cup fresh basil, coarsely chopped

1 Tablespoon raw sugar

2 Tablespoons salt

Fresh ground black pepper to taste

Lemon juice – to use during hot packing process

Instructions

In a large, stainless steel stockpot, combine all ingredients, minus the lemon juice, and bring to a boil over medium-high heat. While stirring, allow to gently boil for 5 minutes to thoroughly blend each flavor.

Jar Prep: Just prior to hot packing, add lemon juice to each empty hot jar: 1 Tablespoon for pints and 2 Tablespoons for quarts.

Add hot basil tomatoes using a slotted spoon, keeping a generous 1" headspace. Ladle in juice from the mixture being sure to maintain headspace.

Wipe each jar rim and screw band with a warm washcloth dipped in vinegar prior to securing lids and rings. Process jars at 10 pounds of pressure; 15 minutes for pints and 20 minutes for quarts.

Alfresco Pasta

Sometimes I do not feel like a heavy meal – especially in the summer months. This lighter alternative to traditional pasta and sauce is the perfect solution. The flavor is robust enough to stand alone atop a bed of fine angel hair pasta.

Ingredients

Individual Portion

Angel Hair Pasta – 2 ounces; dry noodles are 2" circumference totaling 1 cup cooked

1 pint Basil Diced Tomatoes

Sea salt

Extra virgin olive oil

Family Meal

Angel Hair Pasta – dry noodles are 4" in circumference totaling 6 cups cooked

1 quart Basil Diced Tomatoes

Sea salt

Extra virgin olive oil

Instructions

In a medium pot, add Basil Diced Tomatoes. Bring to a boil over medium-high heat, reduce heat and simmer while the pasta cooks.

Using a large pot, be sure to use 10 cups of water when making a family meal. Add two dashes of sea salt and 1 teaspoon of oil to the water and bring it to a full boil. Once water is at a full boil, add pasta and stir well.

Allow water to return to a boil, stirring often to keep the pasta from clumping. Cook the pasta according to the package directions being sure to fish out a noodle every so often to test for doneness. The goal is to cook the pasta al dente – or still firm yet done all the way through. Do not overcook your pasta. When done, drain in colander in sink.

Place angel hair pasta in a bowl, ladle Basil Diced tomatoes atop pasta and serve.

Mixed Bean Medley

Makes approx. 9 quarts or 18 pints

I love adding these mixed beans to soups and stews and often make them a focal point in meal creation. Having a variety of flavors and colors makes a hearty and flavorful refried bean recipe to use in a range of Mexican dishes like wet burritos.

Ingredients

Start with dried, non-GMO beans

Measure accordingly:

3 cups Pinto Beans

2 ½ cups Kidney Beans

2 ¼ cups Black Beans

2 ½ cups Lima Beans

2 ¼ cups Split Peas

2 ½ cups Great Northern Beans

Sea salt (optional)

8-10 cups water

Instructions

This is approximately 6 pounds of dried beans. As with any dried beans, be sure to sort out any disfigured or damaged beans as well as any rocks that may have made it into the bag. Rinse the beans well in a large colander to remove any dirt. Use your hands to turn the beans, ensuring each dried bean receives a thorough washing.

If you would like to add sea salt to your beans, add ¼ teaspoon per pint jar and 1 teaspoon per quart jar prior to filling the jar with dried beans. Salt in this recipe is for flavor and is not required.

Because the pressure canner will cook and soften the beans, there is no need to presoak or precook your dried beans. Using a ladle and funnel, fill each jar ¾ full with clean, dried beans. Next, add water to each jar and fill to 1" headspace. Remove air with air bubble remover tool and adjust headspace with additional water as necessary.

Dip a warm washcloth in vinegar and wipe each jar rim and screw band. Place sterilized lids and rings on each jar and hand tighten. Process in a pressure canner at 10 pounds of pressure; 75 minutes for pints and 90 minutes for quarts.

Sausage & Bean Soup

Makes approx. eight 8-ounce servings

This delicious soup is one of my family's favorites. Packed full of protein and fresh vegetables, this hearty soup gives your family a healthy, filling meal in minutes.

Ingredients

1 quart Mixed Bean Medley

2 quarts Beef Stock

1 ½ pounds Italian sausage

4 carrots, cut into ½" round pieces

1 large onion, diced small

2 celery stalks, cut into ½" pieces

4 garlic cloves, minced

½ bunch kale leaves, stem and main vein removed, chopped course

2 bay leaves

2 Tablespoons extra virgin olive oil

½ teaspoon sea salt – or to taste

¼ teaspoon black pepper – or to taste

Instructions

In a large stockpot combine olive oil, garlic and onions. Sauté on medium heat until onions are softened, about 5 minutes. Add Italian sausage and cook until done, breaking sausage into smaller, bite-size pieces using a wooden spoon. Add beef stock, carrots and celery. Increase heat to medium-high and bring to a boil. Add bay leaves and boil for an additional 5 minutes.

Add Mixed Bean Medley, salt and pepper bringing the soup back to a boil. Once at a boil, reduce heat and simmer for 10 minutes. Add chopped kale and continue to simmer for an additional 5 minutes, stirring occasionally.

Taste-test your soup. If you prefer to add additional salt or pepper feel free to do so, otherwise additional seasonings may be added individually when serving.

Ladle hot soup into bowls. Serve soup alongside a hot slice of beer bread or a handful of oyster crackers.

Ginger Carrots

Makes approx. 6 quarts or 12 pints

Fall is harvest time for your long-awaited root crops! A colorful and healthy favorite in my home is the ever-famous carrot. Turn a boring side dish into something fantastic using a simple addition...ginger! These delicious carrots make a wonderful side dish to complement any dinner. Simply warm on the stove top and serve.

Ingredients

10 pounds carrots, peeled and chopped

1 fresh ginger root – enough to yield 6 teaspoons

Instructions

Wash, peel and wash again the carrots. In my home, we like round, inch-thick pieces – cut according to your preference, making sure they are uniform in size. Have a stockpot of boiling water ready on the stove while chopping.

Wash and peel the ginger root. Using a standard grater, grate the fresh ginger being sure to remove any root fibers. If you would rather, you may simply peel and chop the ginger root into 1" chunks.

Add 1 teaspoon of minced ginger or two chopped pieces to each quart jar and ½ teaspoon to each pint jar. Raw pack carrots tightly leaving 1" of headspace. Ladle boiling water over top of carrots. Remove any excess air bubbles and adjust water level as needed to keep the 1" headspace.

Wipe jar rim with a warm washcloth dipped in vinegar, apply lid and ring. Hand tighten. Process jars at 10 pounds of pressure; 30 minutes for quarts and 25 minutes for pints.

Tip! Use the opposite end of your Headspace Measuring Tool to press down on the carrots to remove trapped air bubbles; then slide the tool down the sides of the jar to remove air pockets. Tamp the jar gently onto the countertop to settle carrots and bring any unseen air bubbles to the surface.

Ginger Carrot Side Dish

Ginger carrots make an excellent side dish straight from the jar. Simply heat through and serve this side as an excellent source of color, nutrients and flavor to any meal. Keep the piece of ginger in the pot while heating through. When serving, remove the ginger or mince fine and sprinkle atop carrots and garnish with parsley.

Ginger Carrot Soup

Makes approx. 4 servings

In addition to making a deliciously simple side dish, turn your home canned carrots into an amazing soup. Easy and filling, this soup is a perfect boost of vitamins and nutrients.

Ingredients

2 Tablespoons butter

1 large onion, chopped

2 celery stalks, chopped

4 garlic cloves, minced

4 sprigs thyme, destemmed

2 quarts Ginger Carrots, drained

6 cups chicken or vegetable stock

1 cup half-and-half

½ teaspoon salt

½ teaspoon pepper

Instructions

In a medium stockpot, add butter, onions, celery, garlic and thyme. Bring to a simmer using medium-high heat, stirring often. Simmer for 6 minutes or until onions are soft and translucent.

Add drained Ginger Carrots, salt, pepper and stock. Bring to a boil on medium-high heat, then reduce heat and simmer for 5 minutes, stirring often. Remove from heat and allow to cool for 5 minutes.

Using your food processor, purée the mixture in small batches, returning puréed soup to a clean stockpot as you go. Using low heat, stir soup while adding half-and-half. Stir well to thoroughly mix ingredients. Remove from heat and serve hot. Garnish with fresh parsley, Parmesan cheese or thin strips of peeled gingerroot.

Naturally Flavored Applesauce

Makes approx. 8 to 10 pints or 4 to 6 quarts

This delicious spin on a traditional favorite gives you and your family a healthy alternative to store bought flavored applesauce. Your kids will love the fun colors the fruits produce in these four easy-to-make options.

Selecting your apples: Using naturally sweet apples like Golden Delicious and Fuji apples gives this sauce the perfect sweetness. If you prefer a tarter applesauce, use Jonathon or Granny Smith apples.

Sugar suggestions: My preference is raw sugar, which is also granulated. Since raw sugar is unbleached, it has a brown hue. White granulated sugar is fine to use in any of my recipes. If you are looking for a lower glycemic sugar, you may use Agave Sweetener. Keep in mind it is very sweet in flavor, so less is more with Agave. If you use Splenda® in your meals to limit sugar intake, you may use Splenda® in equal parts to regular sugar when home canning.

Blueberry Applesauce

12 pounds Golden Delicious or Fuji apples, cored, quartered (skins on)
5 cups blueberries
4 cups water

Cinnamon Applesauce

12 pounds Golden Delicious or Fuji apples, cored, quartered (skins on)
3 Tablespoons ground cinnamon
4 cups water

For each option above:

5 Tablespoons lemon juice
1-3 cups of raw or organic sugar or 1 ½ cups of Agave sweetener (optional)

Instructions

For each option, in a large stockpot combine quartered apples, fruit or cinnamon and water. Bring to a boil over medium-high heat. Reduce heat and boil gently while stirring frequently to avoid scorching. Boil gently for about 15-20 minutes or until apple mixture is tender.

Remove from heat and let cool for about 5 minutes.

Working in batches, transfer apple mixture to a food mill or food processor and purée until smooth. You may also press apple mixture through a chinois.

Pear Applesauce

12 pounds Golden Delicious or Fuji apples, cored, quartered (skins on)
5 pounds pears, skinned, cored and sliced
4 cups water

Strawberry Applesauce

12 pounds Golden Delicious or Fuji apples, cored, quartered (skins on)
7 cups strawberries, hulled and halved
4 cups water

Return purée to a large saucepan and add lemon juice. If you are using sugar or Agave, you may add it now. Bring to a boil over medium-high heat, stirring frequently to avoid scorching.

Hot pack applesauce into hot jars, leaving a ½" of headspace. Remove air bubbles and adjust headspace with more fruit mixture if necessary.

Using a warm washcloth dipped in vinegar, wipe jar rims and screw bands. Add lids and rings and hand tighten. Place jars in water bather, covering the jars with at least an inch of water. Process both pints and quarts for 20 minutes. Remember, processing time doesn't begin until water is a full rolling boil.

Traditional Apple Pie Filling

Makes approx. 7 pint jars

Choose from apples such as Golden Delicious, Fuji, Granny Smith, Jonagold, Lady or Rome Beauty.

Ingredients

Citric Acid Bath: ¼ cup lemon juice mixed with 4 cups of water

Filling Ingredients

12 cups apples, peeled, cored and sliced

2 ¾ cups raw sugar

¾ cup Canning Gel

1 ½ teaspoons ground cinnamon

½ teaspoon ground nutmeg

1 ¼ cups water, cold

2 ½ cups unsweetened apple juice

½ cup lemon juice

Instructions

In a stainless steel bowl, create a citric acid bath. While prepping the apples, plunk apple slices into the citric acid bath to prevent from browning. When done, drain well in a colander being sure to shake off any extra liquid.

In a large, stainless steel stockpot, combine sugar, Canning Gel, cinnamon, nutmeg, water and apple juice. Bring to a boil over medium-high heat being sure to stir constantly to avoid scorching. Cook until mixture thickens and begins to bubble – being sure to stir constantly! Add ½ cup of lemon juice, return to a boil. Set timer and boil for 1 minute, stirring constantly. Remove from heat then immediately fold apple slices into the hot filling. Return to a low heat and stir to ensure the apples are heated through.

Ladle hot pie filling into hot jars, being sure to leave a generous 1" headspace. Remove air bubbles and trapped air pockets and readjust headspace if necessary.

Wipe rims and screw bands with a warm washcloth dipped in vinegar, then add lid and ring. Hand tighten. Process pint jars in a water bath for 25 minutes. Remember, processing time does not begin until water is at a full rolling boil.

Tip!

If you decide to triple or quadruple this recipe it will take twice as long to bring the pie filling to a boil and thicken. To save time, use two (or three) separate stockpots and create no more than a double batch in each pot.

Apple Pie Filling Uses

Having Traditional Apple Pie Filling on hand makes for more than just delicious pies. Although that is reason enough to can apple pie filling. Here are some fun, easy ways to enjoy eating your apple pie filling (or any flavor of your choosing) all year 'round.

À La Mode

Empty a jar of pie filling into a 2-quart saucepan. On medium-high heat, bring filling to a boil stirring often. Remove from heat and serve over vanilla ice cream.

Yogurt Parfait

Take 1 cup of your favorite vanilla or plain yogurt, add heaping 2 Tablespoons of pie filling and top with 2 Tablespoons of granola. If you do not have granola handy, use sliced almonds and raisins.

Apple Brownies

When making a batch of brownies from scratch, add a pint of Traditional Apple Pie filling to the batter.

Apple Pumpkin Bread

After baking a lovely loaf of Pumpkin Bread, allow it to cool before cutting. Cut the entire loaf into ½" thick slices. Lightly grease a 9"x13" glass baking dish and line the bottom of the dish with the loaf slices. Set aside remaining slices. Open 2 pints of home canned Apple Pie filling and spread evenly atop the pumpkin pie slices. Using the slices you have set aside, crumble atop the pie filling. Bake in the oven at 350°F for 15-20 minutes or until heated through.

Canning
Gel

Tart Cherry Pie Filling

Makes approx. 10 pints or 5 quarts

This gorgeous and delicious pie filling makes wonderful pies, tarts and toppings. The beautiful, round cherries and rich filling give way to a lovely gift for any occasion!

Ingredients

10 pounds tart cherries, pitted

3 ½ cups raw sugar

1 cup Canning Gel

1 teaspoon ground cinnamon

¼ cup lemon juice

Instructions

Place a colander atop a large bowl and add all 10 pounds of cherries. Cover colander with a dish towel or cheese cloth to keep pests away. Allow cherries to drain for 2 hours or until you have collected roughly 6 to 8 cups of juice.

Add 4 cups of cherry juice to a large, stainless steel stockpot. Whisk in Canning Gel, sugar and cinnamon. Bring to a boil over medium-high heat being sure to whisk often to avoid scorching. As the mixture begins to bubble add the lemon juice. Set timer and boil for 1 minute being sure to whisk constantly. Add all the cherries at once, return to a boil stirring constantly and gently so the cherries are kept intact. Remove from heat.

Ladle hot pie filling into hot jars leaving a full 1" headspace. Remove any air bubbles and adjust headspace as necessary. Using a warm washcloth dipped in vinegar, wipe jar rims and screw bands. Place sterilized lids and rings atop each jar and hand tighten.

Place jars in water bather and cover with 2" of hot water. Bring to a boil and process pints and quarts for 35 minutes. Remember, do not set your timer until the water has reached a full rolling boil.

Mumma Newton's Dough Recipe

My mumma's dough recipe is handwritten on a tattered recipe card tucked away in her stack of cherished family recipes. Used most of her life, this recipe has fed us many 'a times throughout my life. Use this dough recipe to make pie crusts, pasties, Blonde Goddess desserts and so much more!

To the Table

Ingredients

1 heaping cup of vegetable shortening (my mumma swears by Butter Flavored Crisco®)

A small, stainless steel bowl of ice water with 3 ice cubes

2 cups of flour, heaping

1 teaspoon sea salt, heaping

2 pinches baking powder

Utensils:

Hand sifter

Hand kneader

Rolling pin

Dough rolling mat

Instructions

In a clean bowl, combine flour, salt and baking powder. Working in batches, hand sift the flour mixture into a clean bowl. Set aside.

In a clean large mixing bowl, add 2 Tablespoons shortening and equal parts flour mixture. Knead and blend ingredients. Add an additional 2 Tablespoons of shortening and flour mixture plus 2 Tablespoons of ice water. Knead together. Continue to add shortening and flour mixture in this pattern, only adding additional water to create a slightly sticky consistency. The dough should be in little crumbles. If it becomes too wet or too sticky, lightly dust with flour and knead.

Once all ingredients are kneaded together, using a spatula, pull every bit of dough to the center from the bowl. Form dough into a round ball and place back into the bowl. Cover with plastic wrap and place in refrigerator for 1 hour.

After 1 hour, remove from refrigerator and place on a lightly flour-dusted rolling mat. For pies, use your rolling pin and roll out to ¼" thickness, flipping and maneuvering the dough to create a 10" circle. Use remaining dough to create a top to your pie or have fun using cookie cutters to create shapes to adorn your pie.

CHAPTER 4

Salsas & Chutneys

There are more uses for salsa than on the end of a tortilla chip. Chutney is rarely known and often overlooked, however its uses and flavors are very broad. This chapter will explore fun varieties of both and show you how to use them in meal creation.

Black Bean and Corn Salsa

Makes approx. 6 pints

This salsa is delicious on the end of tortilla chips but very versatile. Use this salsa to replace regular diced tomatoes when making chili and soups. It is also excellent over baked chicken.

Ingredients

8 cups Roma tomatoes, skin on, cored and chopped

1 cup jalapeño peppers, chopped fine

1 cup green bell pepper

1 cup whole kernel corn

1 ½ cups black beans

2 cups red onion, chopped

8 cloves of garlic, minced

½ cup cilantro, chopped and loosely packed

1 Tablespoon of sea salt

½ teaspoon black pepper

¾ cup apple cider vinegar

½ cup fresh lime juice

Instructions

Once each vegetable has been prepped, place all ingredients in a large, stainless steel stockpot and bring to a boil on medium-high heat. Stir often to avoid scorching.

Reduce heat and simmer for 30 minutes. Ladle into hot jars being sure to keep 1/2" headspace. Remove any air bubbles and adjust headspace if necessary. Wipe each jar rim and screw band with a washcloth dipped in vinegar. Add lids and rings, hand tighten.

Place jars in water bather and cover with 2" of water. Process pints for 20 minutes and quarts for 25 minutes. Remember, processing time doesn't begin until water is at a full rolling boil.

Tip!

To get a good ratio of salsa to liquid, use a slotted spoon and fill each pint ¾ full of salsa. Ladle hot salsa liquid into each jar, keeping the required headspace.

Salsa Chicken Bake

Makes approx. 4 to 6 servings

I love using salsa in ways other than just at the end of a tortilla chip. One of my family's favorites is this simple salsa chicken recipe. It is a fast meal when we are all heading off into different directions.

Ingredients

4-6 large boneless skinless chicken breasts

1 cup real mayonnaise

1 pint home canned salsa – I prefer Black Bean & Corn Salsa

3 Tablespoons of real butter

1 cup shredded cheddar cheese

Instructions

Preheat oven to 375°F.

In a medium mixing bowl, combine salsa and mayonnaise. Mix well.

Grease a glass baking dish with butter and place breasts inside. Evenly spread salsa mixture atop the chicken breasts. Cover dish with foil and bake for 30 minutes.

Remove foil and sprinkle with cheese. Bake an additional 10 minutes or until internal temperature of largest portion of the breast reaches 165°F.

Santa Fe Corn Bread

Makes approx. 6 to 8 servings

Talk about an amazing addition to an otherwise traditional bread – you will never eat plain 'ol cornbread again! The best part, you can use with homemade cornbread recipe or simply any boxed bread mix.

Ingredients

1 Tablespoon bacon drippings or real butter

2 cups cornmeal

2 teaspoons baking soda

1 teaspoon salt

1 egg

1 pint Black Bean & Corn Salsa, drained

Instructions

Preheat oven to 400°F.

In a mixing bowl, combine dry ingredients and mix. In a smaller bowl, beat the egg and set aside.

Add drained salsa and egg to the dry ingredients and fold well, but don't over stir. Set aside.

In your cast iron skillet add bacon drippings or butter and melt over medium-high heat. Once melted, turn down to medium so the entire base of the skillet can absorb the heat evenly.

Add the cornbread mixture to the skillet. Using a heat resistant mitt, grab the skillet handle and give it a couple quick shakes to ensure the batter is not high in the center. Place in oven and bake for 20-25 minutes or until the center proves clear when pricking with a butter knife.

Remove from oven and rest on baking rack for 20 minutes before cutting and serving.

Stuffed Bell Peppers

Makes approx. 6 servings

This colorful dish is a show-stopping presentation of flavors and textures served in edible pepper bowls. Kids love the presentation, and the flavor can't be beat.

Ingredients

6 large, flat-bottomed bell peppers – an array of colors

2 teaspoons extra-virgin olive oil

1 pound ground beef – I prefer 80/20 to prevent the rice from drying out

1 medium onion, diced

2 cups cooked rice

1 pint Black Bean & Corn Salsa

1 cup shredded Colby jack and cheddar cheese

Instructions

Preheat oven to 350°F.

Bring a large, stainless steel stockpot of water to a rapid boil to blanch the bell peppers.

Cut the top of each pepper off being sure to leave plenty of base pepper to hold your meal. Remove seeds and membrane. Blanch pepper for 2 minutes in boiling water then dip into a bowl of ice cold water in the sink. Set aside to cool.

Cook rice to package directions and set aside. In a large skillet, add oil and onions and cook on medium-high heat for 5 minutes until translucent. Add ground beef and cook for about 10 minutes or until beef is browned. Add cooked rice, salt and garlic and stir well. Add ¾ of the pint of salsa, stir and heat through.

Stuff each pepper with the meat mixture then place upright in a large glass baking dish. Sprinkle cheese atop each pepper, add a spoonful of salsa atop the cheese then cover with any remaining cheese.

Tent baking dish with foil and bake for 15 minutes. Uncover and bake for an additional 10 minutes or until peppers are tender.

The Diva's Signature Strawberry Salsa

Makes approx. 8 pints

When I created this recipe I was truly looking to flip normal on its head. Who says you can't use fruit in salsa? Not me. And don't get me started on how amazing it tastes! Its bright colors and perfect balance of sweet and heat lend way to its overwhelming popularity.

Ingredients

12 cups of bite-size chopped strawberries (requires about 4 quarts of whole berries)

½ cup Agave sweetener

5 cups of raw, unbleached sugar

1 ¼ cups Vidalia onions, diced

1 cup red onion, diced

1 cup of jalapeño, cut fine – keep seeds if you desire more heat

4 ounces of fresh lime juice

½ cup fresh cilantro, chopped

¾ cup red bell pepper, diced

½ cup green bell pepper, diced

¼ cup fresh mint leaves, finely chopped

1 teaspoon sea salt

1 ¼ cups of apple cider vinegar

Instructions

In a large, stainless steel stockpot on medium-high heat, bring to a boil the sugar, vinegar and agave sweetener. Boil and stir until sugar has dissolved. Add all onions, peppers, herbs, lime juice and spices and bring to a boil. Let boil for 2 minutes then remove from heat. Fold in the cut strawberries. Mix well.

Using a slotted spoon, fill each jar ¾ the way full with salsa. Ladle hot liquid over top of the salsa being sure to keep a ½" headspace.

There will be plenty of liquid left over after filling pints with salsa. Fill additional jars with this delicious liquid keeping the ½" headspace. The liquid makes an excellent marinade and processes the same as the salsa. See Strawberry Salsa Marinade recipes starting on page 131.

Wipe your jar rims with a warm washcloth dipped in vinegar. Add lids and rings atop each jar and hand tighten. Place jars into water bather and cover with 2" of water. Process pint jars for 20 minutes, half-pints for 15 minutes. Remember, processing doesn't begin until the water is at a full rolling boil!

The goal is to achieve a good ratio of solids to liquids in each jar. Using a slotted spoon will help to avoid having supper runny salsa. The key is to fill each jar with solids first then add your liquids. Doing so will help you control the liquid content of the jars.

Berry Spinach

To the Table

Spruce up an average spinach salad with my Signature Strawberry Salsa and a dash (or two) of balsamic vinegar. Need a protein packed lunch? Follow the recipe below, and add your home canned chicken.

Ingredients

Fresh spinach leaves

Strawberry Salsa

Red onion, sliced thin

Fresh cilantro

Balsamic vinegar

Candied pecans (optional)

Instructions

Place a couple handfuls of spinach leaves in the base of a salad bowl. Using a slotted spoon, placed 2 to 3 heaping spoonful's of salsa atop the spinach. Sprinkle red sliced onions atop the leaves – adding as much or as little to suit your preference.

Add 3 to 4 sprigs of cilantro – or if you're like me, I coarsely chop a ¼ cup of leaves and add them to my salad. There really isn't a wrong way to make a salad, so have fun adding candied pecans, sunflower seeds – even a couple fresh strawberries and green apple slices!

Add three dashes of balsamic vinegar and serve.

Strawberry Salsa Cream Cheese Appetizer

To the Table

You will be the talk of the town with this crafty crowd-pleaser! Have unexpected guests and need to serve something in a pinch? Invited to an impromptu get-together? Grab a pint of Strawberry Salsa, a brick of cream cheese and your favorite cracker and away you go.

Ingredients

1 pint Signature Strawberry Salsa

1 brick cream cheese, softened

1 box of your favorite crackers, I love this appetizer with Triscuits® or Pretzel crackers

½ pint fresh strawberries, hulled and halved

Fresh cilantro to garnish, optional

Instructions

Soften a brick of cream cheese on the counter top for 15 minutes. Once softened, place in the center of a serving tray or large plate.

Using a slotted spoon, dish the salsa onto the top of the brick of cream cheese, allowing it to cover the brick and fall some to the sides. Save left over salsa liquid in the refrigerator to make vinaigrette dressing for later. Recipe on page 132.

Serve crackers in a basket alongside the plate being sure to include a knife for spreading.

Strawberry Salsa Pork Dinner

Makes approx. 4 servings

I had so much fun discovering new ways to enjoy eating my Signature Strawberry Salsa. The most fun was using it in main course meal creations. This salsa lightly sweetens the pork while the vinegar tenderizes the meat. Serve your chops alongside a green salad and a side of rice or mashed potatoes.

Ingredients

4 bone-in 1" thick pork chops

1 pint Signature Strawberry Salsa

2 Tablespoons butter

Sea salt and black pepper

Instructions

Preheat oven to 375°F.

In a warm, cast iron skillet, melt butter on medium heat. Brown each side of the pork chop for about a minute being sure to give each side a dash of salt and pepper before flipping.

If using cast iron skillet, leave pork in the skillet. Cover pork chops with Strawberry Salsa and place the skillet in the oven. Otherwise, place pork chops in a glass baking dish and cover with salsa. Regardless of which dish used to bake the chops, allow chops to bake uncovered for 35 minutes or until the juice runs clear in the thickest part of the chop or a thermometer reads a least 145°F.

Remove from oven, lightly tent with foil and allow meat to rest for 5 minutes before serving. Serve additional salsa alongside pork chops.

Signature Strawberry Salsa Marinade

Makes approx. 3 pints

When making the salsa on page 122,
there will be plenty of liquid and salsa particals remaining.

Preserve this delectable marinade to have handy for a variety of uses. Now, depending on whether you doublex or tripled your salsa recipe, you may have enough marinade-filled jars to water bath a full batch in their own water bather.

Instructions

Ladle the remaining liquid from the salsa recipe (page 122) into pint jars being sure to leave ½" headspace.

Wipe your jar rims with a warm washcloth dipped in vinegar, being sure to remove any small salsa particles and residue from the jar rim.

Place sterilized lids and rings atop each jar and hand tighten. Place hot jars into water bather and cover with 2" of water.

Process quarts for 25 minutes, pint jars for 20 minutes, half-pints for 15 minutes. Remember, processing doesn't begin until the water is at a full rolling boil!

Strawberry Vinaigrette

Super simple and packed with sweet flavor! Mix the following in a vinaigrette shaker or whisk together in a shallow bowl. If using a shaker with reliable lid, keep it handy in the refrigerator for up to a month. All you need to do is give it a couple good shakes and pour.

Ingredients

¾ cup Strawberry Salsa Marinade

¼ cup apple cider vinegar

¾ cup extra-virgin olive oil

Instructions

Shaker

Add each ingredient to shaker, close lid and shake well before serving.

Bowl

Whisk each ingredient together and pour into a pint size Mason jar. Stir well before serving. To store, simply add a canning lid and ring and keep refrigerated.

Individual

Only need dressing for a salad or two? No problem. Mix together 1 Tablespoon vinegar, 3 Tablespoons of oil and 3 Tablespoons of marinade.

Marinated Pork Loin

Makes approx. 6 to 8 servings

The flavors in Signature Strawberry Salsa Marinade complement any pork dish and is perfect for injecting! The vinegar and citrus tenderize the pork while the variety of flavors make this loin irresistible. Juicy and tasty, it's unlike any marinade you've tried before! You'll be making more salsa just to keep more of this versatile liquid on hand.

Ingredients

2 pounds pork loin

1 pint Strawberry Salsa Marinade

Meat Injector – preferably one with a dual-sided needle to dispense liquid evenly

Sea salt and black pepper

Instructions

Fill your injector with marinade, trying to leave the bits at the bottom of the jar to avoid clogging the needle. If needed, strain the marinade keeping the bits to later top the loin.

Starting at the top center of the loin, insert the needle 2 inches into the muscle and fill with a half-ounce of marinade. Working to each side, add an additional half-ounce to each side. Repeat this throughout the entire length of the loin being sure not to force the needle all the way through the loin.

Inject up to 8 ounces or half the pint of marinade. Place loin in an air-tight container, pour remaining marinade atop the loin and refrigerate for at least 4 hours. For best results, let marinate overnight.

When ready to bake, preheat oven to 350°F. Remove container from refrigerator and set on your kitchen counter to at allow the loin to get room temperature, about 30 minutes.

Center the loin in a glass baking dish atop a baking rack, dash with salt and pepper then bake uncovered for 50-60 minutes or until internal temperature reaches 150°F. Remove from oven and let rest 10 minutes under tented foil before cutting and serving.

Tangy Pepper Salsa

Makes approx. 5 pints

This amazing salsa hits all the flavors on your palate. It embodies the right amount of heat, sweet and tang, making it the perfect complement to any grilled meat or tortilla chip. Purée this fine mixture and use it as a dipping sauce for chicken tenders, wings or even Asian spring rolls!

Ingredients

6 cups Roma tomatoes, diced

3 cups carrots, peeled and grated

1 cup orange bell pepper

2 cups peaches, peeled and diced

1 ½ cups cider vinegar

1 ¼ cups brown sugar

½ cup onion, finely chopped

½ cup jalapeño peppers, finely chopped – leave seeds for more heat

1 ½ teaspoons sea salt

1 ½ teaspoons fresh ground black pepper

¼ cup cilantro, finely chopped

Instructions

In a large, stainless steel stockpot, combine all ingredients except the cilantro. Bring to a boil over medium heat, stirring often to avoid scorching. Reduce heat and boil gently until mixture starts to thicken, up to one hour. Stir in cilantro and cook for an additional 15 minutes on low heat.

Ladle hot salsa into hot jars leaving ½" headspace. Remove any air bubbles and adjust headspace if necessary. Using a warm washcloth dipped in vinegar, wipe jar rims and screw bands. Add sterilized lid and rings. Hand tighten.

Place jars in water bather and cover with 2" of water. Process pints for 20 minutes, half-pints for 15 minutes. Remember, processing time does not begin until water is at a full rolling boil.

See page 141 for additional options when creating this recipe.

Tangy Huevos

My sister fell in love with my Tangy Pepper Salsa – next thing I know she's adding it to her scrambled eggs at breakfast! The tangy flavors from the salsa give an ordinary egg a wonderful kick.

No matter how you prefer your eggs in the morning, a side of Tangy Pepper Salsa will brighten your day. Me? I love my eggs sunny side up. Simple. Delicious. Perfection.

Ingredients

2 fresh eggs

2 teaspoons real butter

Sea salt and black pepper

1 pint Tangy Pepper Salsa

Instructions

Crack two eggs into a small bowl. Set aside. In a non-stick skillet, melt butter over medium-low heat.

When the butter has melted and begins to bubble, gently pour the egg into the skillet. Cook until the whites are opaque and each yolk has set, about 2 minutes. Dash each egg with salt and pepper.

Plate each egg and serve with 2 Tablespoons of salsa and a fresh glass of orange juice.

Tangy Pepper Dipping Sauce

Makes approx. 5 pints

Although Tangy Pepper Salsa recipe is located on page 137, this fun recipe gives you two variations; you can follow the instructions below, so you may preserve it as a dipping sauce and not a salsa. Or, you may simply purée the salsa prior to serving. Either way, you can't go wrong – the uses for this delicious dipping sauce are endless! My canning students tell me they even used Tangy Pepper Dipping Sauce in their Bloody Mary mix.

To the Jar

Ingredients

Use all ingredients listed on page 137

½ cup Canning Gel

Instructions

In a large, stainless steel stockpot, combine all ingredients except the cilantro. Bring to a boil over medium heat, stirring often to avoid scorching. Reduce heat and boil gently until mixture starts to thicken, up to one hour. Stir in cilantro and cook for an additional 15 minutes on low heat.

Using a food processor and working in batches, purée the salsa until it reaches a fine consistency. Do not liquefy. Return to a large stockpot on medium-high heat and bring to a boil, being sure to stir often to avoid scorching the sauce. Whisk in the Canning Gel, whisking until dissolved. Return to a boil, then reduce heat and simmer for 5 additional minutes, stirring often.

Ladle hot salsa into hot jars leaving ½" headspace. Remove any air bubbles and adjust headspace if necessary. Using a warm washcloth dipped in vinegar, wipe jar rims and screw bands. Add sterilized lid and rings. Hand tighten.

Place jars in water bather and cover with 2" of water. Process pints for 20 minutes, half-pints for 15 minutes. Remember, processing time does not begin until water is at a full rolling boil.

Diane's Traditional Salsa

Makes approx. 6 pints

I could eat this salsa for breakfast, lunch and dinner! It truly is simple and flavorful. I will often use a pint of traditional salsa rather than plain, diced tomatoes to give my recipe a flavor-kick.

Ingredients

8 cups Roma tomatoes, skin on, cored and chopped

1 cup jalapeño peppers, chopped fine

1 cup green bell pepper

2 cups red onion, chopped

8 cloves of garlic, minced

½ cup cilantro, chopped

1 Tablespoon sea salt

½ teaspoon black pepper

¾ cup apple cider vinegar

½ cup fresh lime juice

Instructions

Once each vegetable has been prepped, place all ingredients in a large, stainless steel stockpot and bring to a boil on medium-high heat. Stir often to avoid scorching.

Reduce heat and simmer for 30 minutes. Ladle into hot jars being sure to keep ½" headspace. Remove any air bubbles and adjust headspace if necessary. Wipe jar rims and screw bands with a washcloth dipped in vinegar. Add sterilized lids and rings and hand tighten.

Place jars in water bather and cover with 2" of water. Process pints for 20 minutes and quarts for 25 minutes. Remember, processing time doesn't begin until water is at a full rolling boil.

Zesty Tomato Salsa

Makes approx. 12 8-ounce jars or 6-7 pints

This salsa goes above and beyond any traditional tomato salsa blend! Replacing jalapeños with poblano peppers and red wine vinegar over apple cider vinegar, the flavors just dance in your mouth!

To the Jar

Ingredients

9-12 dried California Chili Peppers

4 cups boiled water

12 cups finely diced Roma tomatoes, skin on

3 cups finely chopped red onions

1 ½ cups finely chopped cilantro

15 cloves of garlic, minced

3 large Poblano Peppers, cored and chopped fine

¾ cup red wine vinegar

1 Tablespoon sea salt

¾ teaspoon red pepper flakes

Instructions

Use your food processor and pulse each ingredient or hand chop fine. Be careful not to purée the ingredients as there should be some texture to the salsa. The rehydrated chili peppers are the only ingredient you will purée in this recipe.

Dried Chili Pepper Prep: Remove the stems and a portion of the seeds. Keeping some seeds is okay and will add to the salsa's texture and flavor. Using a small, stainless steel stockpot, place your dried chili peppers inside and cover with boiling hot water. To fully submerge the peppers, use a salad plate atop the peppers and rest a soup bowl full of hot water on top of the plate. The peppers need to be fully submerged for 20 minutes to rehydrate.

While the chili peppers are rehydrating, finely chop (or pulse in food processor) and measure the remaining ingredients. After the chilies have rehydrated, place them in your food processor with a ¼ cup of the chili water to reconstitute. Purée the chili peppers and water until a paste is created.

In a large, stainless steel stockpot, combine all ingredients and mix well. Bring to a boil over medium-high heat, stirring often to avoid scorching the salsa. Once brought to a boil, reduce heat and simmer for 10 minutes. Ladle hot salsa into hot jars, leaving a ½" of headspace. Use a warm washcloth dipped in vinegar to wipe the jar rims and screw bands. Place prepared lids and rings atop each jar and hand tighten. Process jars in a hot water bath, 15 minutes for pints and 20 minutes for quarts. Remember, processing time doesn't begin until water is at a full rolling boil.

Rhubarb Apple Chutney

Makes approx. 7 half-pints

This gorgeous chutney has a tart yet sweet flavor and warm tones, making it perfect for scones, crepes and pastry fillings. It is also delicious alongside pork as well as a cheese and fruit tray.

Ingredients

5 cups apples, peeled, diced and cored

4 cups rhubarb, diced

4 cups raw sugar

Zest of 1 lemon

2 Tablespoons lemon juice

1 cup dried cranberries, packed

1 teaspoon ground cinnamon

1 teaspoon ground nutmeg

Instructions

In a large, stainless steel stockpot, combine apples, sugar and rhubarb. On medium heat, bring to a boil and simmer, stirring frequently, for 15 minutes. Add cranberries, cinnamon and nutmeg. Continue to boil gently to reduce down the mixture, for 15 additional minutes.

Ladle hot chutney into sterilized, hot jars leaving a ½" of headspace. Remove air bubbles and adjust headspace if necessary. Using a warm washcloth dipped in vinegar, wipe jar rim and screw bands. Apply sterilized lids and rings. Hand tighten.

Place jars in water bather and cover with 1" of water. Process half-pints for 10 minutes, pints for 15 minutes. Remember, processing time does not begin until water is at a full rolling boil.

Beef Tenderloin with Rhubarb Chutney and Spicy Mustard

Makes approx. 4 to 6 servings

A quick, simple meal in no time! Follow these steps to create the perfect steak and side dish on the stovetop.

Ingredients

2 Tablespoons extra-virgin olive oil

2 Tablespoons real butter

4 to 6 beef tenderloin steaks or medallions

Pink Himalayan sea salt

Cracked black pepper

1 pound Brussels sprouts, cleaned and cut in half

3 garlic cloves, chopped course

Favorite stone ground mustard

1 half-pint Rhubarb Apple Chutney

Instructions

Remove the tenderloins from the refrigerator 30 minutes before cooking to bring them to room temperature. Pat the tenderloins with a paper towel. Sprinkle generously with Himalayan sea salt and fresh ground pepper being sure to press the seasonings into each side of the meat.

Using a cast iron skillet, add 1 Tablespoon of oil and heat using high heat. Move the oil about the pan to adequately cover the surface the steaks will contact. Sear the steaks for two to three minutes on each side.

Add 1 Tablespoon of butter to the skillet, turn heat down to medium and cook for 10 additional minutes, being sure to flip the steaks so each side cooks consistently. Depending on how you like to eat your steaks, remove them from the skillet 5°F before your desired temperature. Set aside to rest for 12-15 minutes, tenting foil atop the steaks to keep the heat.

Add the remaining butter and oil. On medium-high heat, scrape the drippings and bits from the pan and add Brussels sprouts and garlic. Stir to coat well. Add 2 Tablespoons of water and cover half the pan with a lid allowing some moisture to escape. Cook Brussels sprouts for 5-6 minutes then stir. Cook for an additional 8 minutes, stirring as needed. Plate your steak and Brussel sprouts first, and then add 2-3 Tablespoons of chutney alongside the steak and a dapple of mustard near the sprouts.

Pear & Rhubarb Tarte Tatin

Give depth and texture to your tarte tatin with Rhubarb Apple Chutney. Complemented with warm undertones of cinnamon and allspice, this amazingly easy and scrumptious dessert is sure to please. Serve warm – and if handy, add a small scoop of vanilla ice cream atop each plated piece.

Ingredients

3 Tablespoons butter

2 large Bartlett pears, peeled

2 rhubarb stalks, ends removed

1 half-pint jar Rhubarb Apple Chutney

Mumma Newton's Pie Dough – or refrigerated store-bought dough

A serving plate, equal to or larger than the circumference of the skillet

Instructions

Preheat oven to 350°F.

Slice each pear into four even lengthwise pieces, cutting straight through the core. Using a paring knife, remove the core and seeds from the two center slices and discard. Cut the rhubarb into 2 ½ inch slices. Wider stalks may be cut in half then cut to length.

In a 10" oven-safe skillet, melt butter on medium heat, being sure to coat the entire base of the skillet with the melted butter. Arrange the pears and rhubarb in an every-other sequence. The design you make in the skillet will represent the top of the tarte tatin.

Reduce heat to a low and cook for 10 minutes. Using a tablespoon, fill in the gaps surrounding the rhubarb and pears with the chutney. Be sure to use the entire half-pint. Cook for an additional 3 minutes.

Place the pie dough atop of the fruit/chutney, lightly tucking each edge into the sides of the skillet. Bake for about 30-40 minutes or until the pie dough is a golden brown.

Remove the skillet from the oven and rest on the stove top. Wearing heat-proof mitts, place the plate atop the skillet. With the palm of your hand firmly pressed in the center of the plate, lift the skillet by its handle with your other hand. In one fluid motion, lift up and flip the skillet onto the plate – pausing for a couple seconds before removing the skillet.

Kiwi Chutney

Kiwi Chutney

Makes approx. 9 half-pints or 5 pints

This savory chutney embodies warm tones and sweet hues of fruit flavor which work well alongside a main dish or served as an appetizer. It makes a delicious accompaniment to meats, is excellent served with a cheese and cracker tray and will wow guests when heated and served atop goat cheese garnished with apple and kiwi slices.

Ingredients

6 cups kiwi, peeled and chopped

3 Granny Smith apples, peeled, cored and chopped

1 cup onion, chopped

1 ½ cups apple cider vinegar

1 ½ cups raw sugar

¾ cup brown sugar, packed

1 cup golden raisins

6 garlic cloves, chopped fine

1 teaspoon gingerroot, peeled and finely chopped

1 teaspoon ground cinnamon

1 teaspoon ground allspice

½ teaspoon cayenne pepper

½ teaspoon ground cloves

1 teaspoon mustard seeds

¼ teaspoon sea salt

¼ teaspoon black pepper

Instructions

In a large, stainless steel stockpot, combine ingredients and bring to a boil over medium-high heat being sure to stir constantly to avoid scorching. Reduce heat and boil gently for 30 minutes while stirring frequently. Be sure to monitor the heat as chutney thickens so it does not scorch.

Ladle hot chutney into hot jars, leaving a ½" of headspace. Remove any air bubbles and adjust headspace if necessary. Use a warm washcloth dipped in vinegar, wipe the jar rims and screw bands. Add sterilized lids and rings atop each jar and hand tighten.

Place jars in a water bath and cover with an inch of water. Process half-pints for 10 minutes and pints for 15 minutes. Remember, processing time doesn't begin until water is at a full rolling boil.

Kiwi Chutney Glazed Beef

Makes approx. 6 servings

Use your home canned goods to turn an ordinary pot roast into something extraordinary! This impressive chutney is the perfect complement to beef with its touch of cayenne pepper.

Ingredients

3 pound beef roast, eye of round

2 Tablespoons extra virgin olive oil

1 pint Kiwi Chutney

Sea salt and black pepper

4 potatoes, cleaned and quartered

1 large onion, quartered

2 garlic cloves, halved lengthwise

Instructions

Prior to preparing the roast, remove it from the refrigerator and set on the counter top for 40-45 minutes allowing the meat to acclimate to room temperature. Preheat oven to 375°F.

Remove roast from packaging and pat dry with a paper towel. Using a large skillet on high heat, add olive oil and flash sear each side of the beef roast. Set roast in center of roasting pan. Dash with sea salt and black pepper. Spread half the pint of chutney onto the top of the beef roast. Place potatoes and onions around the roast. Sprinkle garlic cloves atop the roast and vegetables.

Cover and roast for 20 minutes per pound or until internal temperature reaches 135°F. Remove from oven and let rest 15 minutes before cutting as the internal temperature will increase by 10 degrees, giving you a slightly pink center and plenty of juiciness. Slice thin and serve with the remaining half of chutney.

Savory Cherry Chutney

Makes approx. 12 half-pint or 6 pint jars

Use this delicious chutney on any cheese and meat tray and WOW your guests with its amazing array of flavors. Savory Cherry Chutney complements any meal beautifully and its uses are endless.

Ingredients

10 cups sweet cherries, pitted and coarsely chopped

2 large baking apples, peeled and chopped fine

1 ½ cups raisins

1 ½ cups of sweet onion, cut in half then sliced thin

1 cup apple cider vinegar

4 garlic cloves, peeled and finely chopped

2 Tablespoons Agave sweetener

½ cup raw sugar

½ teaspoon sea salt

¼ teaspoon black pepper

1 Tablespoon mustard seeds

1 teaspoon ground allspice

Instructions

Using a skillet and wooden spoon, on low heat gently sauté the sliced onions in the Agave sweetener until caramelized. Approximately 7-10 minutes. Lightly dust with black pepper, stir and set aside.

In a large stockpot, combine all ingredients including the caramelized onions and bring to a boil using medium-high heat. Stir often to avoid scorching. Boil gently for 5 minutes then fill clean, warm jars leaving a ½" of headspace. Remove air bubbles and adjust headspace as necessary.

With a warm washcloth dipped in vinegar, wipe each jar rim thoroughly to remove any food debris. Place lids and rings atop each jar and hand tighten. Place jars in a water bather and cover with 1" of hot water. Process jars in a hot water bath, 10 minutes for half-pints and 15 minutes for pints. Remember, processing time doesn't begin until water is at a full rolling boil.

Stuffed Chicken Breasts

Makes approx. 4 servings

Serving chicken for dinner is a norm in many households – and although healthy, it can get mundane quickly. Change things up by stuffing each breast with home canned Savory Cherry Chutney. Add a bit of Parmesan cheese and enjoy!

Ingredients

4 boneless, skinless chicken breasts

1 pint Savory Cherry Chutney

¾ cup shredded Parmesan cheese

2 Tablespoons extra-virgin olive oil

Instructions

Preheat oven to 375°F.

In a large skillet on medium-high heat, add oil and chicken breasts. Brown both sides of the breast fully, about 4 minutes on each side. Remove from heat and set aside on a cutting board to cool.

In a small bowl, mix chutney and ½ cup cheese.

When breasts are cool to touch, slit a long pocket on the side of the breast, being sure not to cut all the way through the breast. The goal is to cut long and deep, staying an inch away from the sides of the breast. Use your fingers to create a pocket to insert the chutney mixture.

Using a tablespoon, fill each pocket with at least 2 Tablespoons of chutney mixture. Seal pocket closed with toothpicks. Place each stuffed breast in an ungreased glass baking dish.

Bake for 30 minutes or until juice runs clear from breasts. Remove toothpicks, sprinkle with remaining cheese and serve hot.

Blonde Curry Apple Chutney

Makes approx. 6 pint jars

This chutney embodies vibrant Indian flavors...ginger and allspice are a beautiful addition to chicken or pork. It is gorgeous in color, boasting shades of blonde.

Ingredients

4 cups white vinegar

8 cups Golden Delicious or Spartan apples – peeled, cored and chopped

5 ½ cups golden raisins

4 cups raw granulated sugar

1 cup onions, chopped

1 cup sweet bell pepper, chopped and seeded

2 jalapeño peppers, chopped

3 garlic cloves, finely chopped

3 Tablespoons mustard seeds

2 Tablespoons ground ginger

2 teaspoons ground allspice

3 teaspoons yellow curry powder

2 teaspoons sea salt

3 garlic cloves, finely chopped

Instructions

In a large, stainless steel stockpot, add white vinegar. As you are prepping your apples, place them in the vinegar, giving them a quick stir so that the vinegar coats the apples to prevent them from browning. Add golden raisins, sugar, onion and red pepper. Bring to a boil over medium-high heat, stirring frequently, for 30 minutes. Add mustard seeds, ginger, allspice, curry, salt, peppers and garlic. Boil gently, stirring frequently, until thick enough to mound on a spoon – approximately 15 minutes.

Ladle hot chutney into hot jars leaving a ½" headspace. Remove any air bubbles adjusting headspace if necessary. Wipe rim using a warm washcloth dipped in vinegar, then add sterilized lid and ring. Hand tighten.

Process pint jars in a water bath for 15 minutes. Remember, processing time does not begin until water is at a full rolling boil.

Blonde Goddess Mini Pies

Makes approx. 8 servings

Include the kiddos when making this fun appetizer. We often consider these a healthy dessert too! In a pinch for time? No worries! You can use refrigerated store-bought pie dough, pop open a jar of Blonde Curry Apple Chutney and let little hands enjoy scooping and filling their "mini pie."

Ingredients

1 pint Blonde Curry Apple Chutney

8 ounces of Brie cheese

15 ounces of pastry dough (either store-bought or homemade)

1 apple, cored and sliced

Instructions

If using homemade dough, roll the dough until ¼" thick on a lightly floured surface. Create eight 5" triangle or round shapes. Place 2 Tablespoons of chutney in the center of the dough. Cut the Brie cheese into 8 evenly shaped pieces. Place a piece of Brie atop each mini-pie.

Lift the edges of the dough and pinch atop the mixture to seal. Place on a non-stick cookie sheet and bake at 350° for 15-20 minutes or until the pastry dough is golden brown. It is normal for some cheese and chutney to ooze outside the dough.

Remove from oven and allow to sit for 3 minutes. Place individual pies onto a serving plate and garnish with two apple slices, a slice of Brie or raisins. Serve warm.

Blonde Brie Bake

Makes approx. 8 servings

A simple yet delicious precursor to any meal, Blonde Brie Bake is a crowd pleaser. The creaminess of the Brie blends beautifully with the curry undertones and sweet blonde raisins. Serve with apple slices and water crackers. A perfect appetizer any time of the year.

Ingredients

1 pint Blonde Curry Apple Chutney

16 ounces Brie cheese – I often use Président® cheese

1 apple, cored and cut into thin slices

1 box water cracker or biscuit – any thin, crispy cracker will work

Instructions

Preheat oven to 350°F.

Empty the chutney into a 2-quart saucepan and bring to a gentle boil over medium-high heat. Stir often to evenly distribute heat. When warmed through, set aside.

Place a sheet of parchment or wax paper onto a cookie sheet. Center Brie onto the paper and bake in the oven for 7 minutes. Remove from oven, dump warm chutney all over the top of the Brie and spread evenly. Bake for an additional 3-5 minutes or until the Brie just starts to ooze.

Using a large spatula, gently lift the Brie off the wax paper and onto the center of your serving plate. If you accidentally puncture the Brie, not to worry. Surround the Brie with apple slices and water crackers and serve warm.

Blonde Chutney Stuffed Pork Loin

The delicious blend of curry and allspice give pork a delectable flavor and juiciness that is out of this world. A dish sure to impress, its simplicity makes it easy to serve for any occasion.

Ingredients

1 pint Blonde Curry Apple Chutney

1 ½ pound pork loin

Butchers twine

Black pepper and sea salt

6" boning knife

Instructions

Preheat oven at 375°F.

On a large cutting board, starting at the right side of the loin, insert your knife at a ½" thickness from the edge and cut lengthwise. The goal is to work your way around the exterior of the loin, turning the pork loin one rotation to continue to open the loin. Be sure not to cut all the way through the entire pork loin. On the final rotation, continue to work the knife gently lengthwise until the loin is cut flat. The outcome is to butterfly and open the loin, creating a flat surface to stuff the chutney.

Using a meat mallet, pound the loin until it is about ¼" to ½" thick. Be careful not to over pound any particular area causing holes or tears in the muscle.

Spread the chutney atop the loin keeping it 1 inch from the edge. Starting on the short side, roll the loin pulling and tucking the chutney and meat inward. Any chutney that escapes simply add into the next roll or slather onto the outside of the loin.

Using butchers twine, tie the center of the roll tightly to keep it intact. Tie each end then tie any additional areas that require securing. Dash the exterior with salt and pepper and place into baking dish.

Roast for 1 hour or until internal temperature reaches 150°F and juices run clear. Remove from the oven and let rest 10 minutes before removing twine and cutting.

Serve alongside a fresh spinach salad and creamed sweet potatoes. Recipe on page 86.

CHAPTER 5

Pickling & Fermentation

Learn an age-old canning technique with The Canning Diva®! While dill pickles are perhaps the most common pickle, the scope of home-canned vegetable pickles is endless!

Dilled Baby Carrots

Makes approx. 7 to 8 pints

Who says pickles need to be green? Enjoy these fresh out of the jar or on a skewer in your Bloody Mary! Either way they are sure to delight!

Ingredients

6 cups white vinegar

2 cups water

½ cup pickling or canning salt

4 cloves of garlic, cut in half or if small whole

14 heads of dill or ½ teaspoon of dill seeds per jar

3 ½ teaspoons hot pepper flakes

5 pounds baby carrots or regular sized carrots with ends removed, peeled and cut into 2" long sticks

Instructions

Brine: In a large, stainless steel stockpot, combine vinegar, water and salt. Stir well and bring to a boil, continuing to stir to dissolve the salt. Boil for 1 minute then remove from heat.

Place a half garlic clove in each jar, 1 head of dill or ½ teaspoon of dill seeds and a ½ teaspoon of hot pepper flakes if you are using them. Raw pack the carrots into each jar leaving a ½" headspace.

Ladle hot brine into jars being sure to maintain the ½" headspace. Remove any air bubbles using your canning utensil or the handle of a wooden spoon. Adjust headspace if necessary.

Using a warm washcloth dipped in vinegar, wipe each rim and screw bands. Place lids and rings on each jar and hand tighten.

Place jars in water bather and cover with 1" of water. Process the jars for 10 minutes. Remember, processing time doesn't begin until the water is at a full rolling boil.

Tip!

If you run out of brine, make a half batch of brine, boil and fill jars accordingly. Never fill your remaining jars with just water – it will lessen the acidic level and cause food to spoil.

Pickled Ramps

Makes 6 half-pints

The ramp, also called a wild leek, is a wild onion native to North America. The bulb resembles that of a scallion and the leaves are broad, flat and beautiful! Ramps can be pickled or used in place of cooking onions and garlic.

Ingredients

3 pounds of ramps

Brine

3 ¾ cups white vinegar

3 cups water

3 Tablespoons pickling salt

6 Tablespoons honey

Seasonings Per Jar

¼ teaspoon mustard seeds

¼ teaspoon whole coriander seeds

2-3 whole black peppercorns

1 dried bay leaf

Instructions

Thoroughly wash and cut your ramps. Cut the bulb just above the white, allowing some burgundy stem to remain, which is also known as the taproot. Be sure to keep the green leaves to use in soups, sauces or see my dehydration recipe on page 33 to keep as a dried herb when cooking.

In a large, stainless steel stockpot, combine vinegar, water, salt honey to create the brine. Stir well to dissolve the salt and honey and bring to a boil. Let boil for 1 minute then remove from heat.

Place the specified seasonings into each jar. Raw pack the ramps tightly leaving a ½" headspace. Ladle hot liquid into jars being sure to maintain the ½" headspace. Remove any air bubbles and adjust headspace as necessary.

Using a warm washcloth dipped in vinegar, wipe each rim and screw bands. Place lids and rings on each jar and hand tighten.

Place jars in water bather and cover with water. Process the jars for 15 minutes. Remember, processing time doesn't begin until the water is at a full rolling boil.

Tip! If you run out of pickling liquid, make a half batch of brine, boil and fill jars accordingly. Never fill your remaining jars with just water – it will lessen the acidic level and cause the food to spoil.

Pickled Ramp Martini

Makes 1 cocktail

For those of you who love plunking a pearl onion in your martini, this recipe is for you! The amazing blend of coriander and garlic coupled with the hint of honey from the brine make an otherwise boring martini new and exciting. It's earthy but sweet flavor will be your new found favorite.

Ingredients

2 ½ ounces your favorite vodka

Jar of Pickled Ramps

¼ ounce Pickled Ramp juice, less or more, depending on your preference

½ ounce vermouth

Fresh cracked black pepper

Instructions

Place one or two pickled ramps in a chilled martini glass.

Fill a martini shaker with ice. Add vodka, your preferred amount of ramp juice (dirty to your liking) and vermouth into the shaker.

Shake very well – up to 45 shakes – the longer the better since you cannot over shake this cocktail.

Strain into the martini glass atop the pickled ramp.

Crack two turns of fresh black pepper overtop the cocktail and serve.

Pickled Asparagus

Makes approx. eight 8-ounce jars or 4 pints

This is the best alternative to a standard pickle – especially when asparagus is in full season. Have fun munching on these crunchy treats alongside a frothy beer or complement by a sandwich and chips.

Ingredients

7 pounds asparagus

5 cups white vinegar

5 cups water

½ cup pickling or canning salt

6 cloves of garlic, whole

Dill seed or fresh dill flower sprig

Mustard seed

Crushed red pepper flakes (optional)

Instructions

Brine: In a large, stainless steel stockpot, combine vinegar, water and salt. Stir well and bring to a boil, stirring to dissolve the salt.

Remove tough ends from asparagus. Place a garlic clove, ½ teaspoon dill seeds (or 1 fresh dill flower sprig), ½ teaspoon of hot pepper flakes (optional) and ½ teaspoon mustard seeds in each jar. Raw pack the asparagus into each jar, leaving a generous ½" headspace.

Ladle hot liquid into jars being sure to maintain the ½" headspace. Remove any air bubbles and adjust headspace is necessary.

Using a warm washcloth dipped in vinegar, wipe each rim and screw bands. Place lids and rings on each jar and hand tighten.

Place jars in water bather and cover with 1" of water. Process the jars for 10 minutes. Remember, processing time doesn't begin until the water is at a full rolling boil.

Tip!

If you run out of pickling liquid, make a half batch of brine, boil and fill jars accordingly. Never fill your remaining jars with just water – it will lessen the acidic level and cause food to spoil.

Pickled Brussels Sprouts

Makes approx. 10 to 12 half-pints or 5 to 6 pints

Keep 'em dilled or add a bit of heat using hot pepper flakes. Serving a relish tray for the holidays? Add these round beauties to impress your guests.

Ingredients

6 cups white vinegar

2 cups water

½ cup pickling or canning salt

3 cloves of garlic, cut in half or if small whole

14 heads of fresh dill or ½ teaspoon of dill seeds per jar

½ teaspoon hot pepper flakes per jar (optional – I like to make half the jars spicy and the other regular)

3 pounds Brussels sprouts

Instructions

Brine: In a large, stainless steel stockpot, combine vinegar, water and salt. Stir well and bring to a boil, stirring to dissolve the salt.

Cut ends of Brussels sprouts and remove outer layer of sprout leaves, then rinse. Place a half garlic clove in each jar, 1 head of dill or ½ teaspoon of dill seeds and a ½ teaspoon of hot pepper flakes if you are using them. Raw pack the the Brussels sprouts into each jar leaving a generous ½" headspace.

Ladle hot liquid into jars being sure to maintain the ½" headspace. Remove any air bubbles using your canning utensil or the handle of a wooden spoon. Adjust headspace is necessary.

Using a warm washcloth dipped in vinegar, wipe each rim and screw bands. Place lids and rings on each jar and hand tighten.

Place jars in water bather and cover with 1" of water. Process the jars for 10 minutes. Remember, processing time doesn't begin until the water is at a full roiling boil.

Tip!

If you run out of pickling liquid, make a half batch of brine, boil and fill jars accordingly. Never fill your remaining jars with just water – it will lessen the acidic level and cause food to spoil.

Pickled Garlic Cloves

Makes approx. 5 to 6 half-pints

Add these beauties to pasta whole or you may simply mash the cloves to create a paste that can be spread over a baguette. And, for those of you who love a spicy Bloody Mary, plunk a couple of these bad boys in your glass and let the flavors explode!

Ingredients

2 ½ cups white vinegar

1 cup Pinot Grigio

1 Tablespoon pickling or canning salt

1 Tablespoon raw sugar

1 ½ Tablespoons dried oregano

12-15 large garlic heads, separated and peeled

Jar Prep:

5-6 dried California Dried Chilies

2 Tablespoons dried oregano

Instructions

Be sure jars are setting in hot water as this method of jar filling is via hot packing.

Brine: In a large, stainless steel stockpot, combine vinegar, wine, sugar, 1 teaspoon oregano and salt. Stir well and bring to a boil, stirring to dissolve the sugar and salt. Reduce heat and let boil gently for 1 minute. Set a timer; do not guess. Add peeled garlic cloves and cook for 1 minute more.

Place a pinch of oregano and 1 dried chili pepper into each hot jar. Feel free to cut a pepper in half as they can be long. Using a slotted spoon and funnel, fill each jar with garlic cloves, leaving a generous ½" headspace. Using a ladle, fill each jar with brine being sure to keep the generous ½" headspace. Remove any air bubbles and adjust headspace if necessary.

Using a warm washcloth dipped in vinegar, wipe each rim and screw bands. Place lids and rings on each jar and hand tighten.

Place jars in water bather and cover with 1" water. Process the jars for 10 minutes. Remember, processing time doesn't begin until the water is at a full rolling boil.

Pickled Serrano Peppers

Makes 10 to 12 half-pints or 5 to 6 pints

Excellent straight out of the jar or atop a homemade pizza! You can't go wrong with these little beauties. This recipe is a remarkable solution for home grown peppers whose yield was much greater than expected! Give them a try – you won't be disappointed.

Ingredients

50-60 Serrano peppers

6 cups white vinegar

2 cups water

½ cup pickling or canning salt

3 cloves of garlic, cut in half or if small whole

2 Tablespoons whole black peppercorns

2 Tablespoons coriander seeds

1 teaspoon cumin seeds

2 bay leaves

Instructions

Brine: In a large, stainless steel stockpot, combine vinegar, water and salt. Stir well and bring to a boil, stirring to dissolve the salt. Add garlic cloves, dried herbs and spices and return to a boil. Boil for 2 minutes to allow the seasonings to permeate the brine. Remove bay leaves and remove from heat.

Tightly raw pack the peppers, stems and all into each jar, leaving a generous ½" headspace. Be sure to fill every nook and cranny of space in the jar. Using tongs, retrieve a half garlic clove from the brine and place one in each jar.

Ladle hot brine atop peppers being sure to maintain a generous ½" headspace. Remove any air bubbles and adjust headspace as necessary. Using a warm washcloth dipped in vinegar, wipe each rim and screw band. Place lids and rings on each jar and hand tighten.

Place jars in water bather and cover with 1" of water. Process the jars for 10 minutes. Remember, processing time doesn't begin until the water is at a full rolling boil.

The Canning
DIVA
Serrano Peppers
8/11
www.canningdiva.com

Pickled Beets and Onions

Makes approx. 6 pint jars

One of my favorite snacks growing up as a child! I will always remember my mom using her favorite 1 gallon canning jar in her bright yellow kitchen. She would make a large batch of pickled beets and onions, and later would add hard-boiled eggs after popping the top. By adding eggs she would keep this jar of goodness in the fridge, so we could enjoy this yummy snack any time!

Ingredients

Cheesecloth and string

3 Tablespoons pickling spice

2 ½ cups white vinegar

1 cup water

1 cup raw sugar

10 cups of prepared beets; approx. 10 to 12 beets will yield 10 cups

2 large Vidalia onions

Instructions

Using a 4" square piece of cheesecloth, place the pickling spice in the center. Tie together using string to create a spice bag.

Beet Prep: Cut stems leaving 2" and keep the root. Blanch for 30 minutes in boiling water. Cool in bowl of cold water in the sink. Under a cold stream of water, use thumbs and slide skin off beat. On cutting board, remove stem and root. Quarter large beets and leave smaller beets whole – be sure to keep beets uniform in size.

In a large, stainless steel stockpot, combine vinegar, water, sugar, onions and spice bag. Bring to a boil over medium heat. Stir until sugar has dissolved and boil gently for about 15 minutes. After 15 minutes, remove the spice bag and discard. Add prepared beets and return to a boil.

Using a slotted spoon, ladle beets into hot jar leaving a generous ½" headspace. Ladle hot pickling liquid over beets, being sure to cover them and maintain the headspace. Remove air bubbles and adjust headspace using hot liquid as necessary.

Wipe jar rim and screw bands using a warm washcloth dipped in vinegar. Place lid and rings on and hand tighten. Process pints in a water bath for 30 minutes. Remember, processing time doesn't begin until water is at a full rolling boil.

300
200
100

Dilly Beans

Makes approx. 6 to 8 pints

Excellent in a salad, as an addition to a relish tray or fresh right out of the jar, just like a pickle!

Ingredients

7 pounds green beans; often I will mix 3.5 pounds of yellow wax beans with green beans

5 cups white vinegar

5 cups water

½ cup pickling or canning salt

6–8 cloves of garlic, whole

Dill seed or 8 fresh dill flower sprigs

Mustard seed

Crushed red pepper flakes (optional)

Instructions

Brine: In a large, stainless steel stockpot, combine vinegar, water and salt. Stir well and bring to a boil, continuing to stir to dissolve the salt.

Rinse beans in a colander and remove any discolored and disfigured beans from the lot. Using a cutting board and paring knife, remove the stem ends.

Place one garlic clove, ½ teaspoon dill seeds (or 1 fresh dill flower sprig), ½ teaspoon mustard seeds in each jar and ½ teaspoon of hot pepper flakes (optional) in each jar. Raw pack cleaned and prepped beans tightly into each jar leaving a generous ½" headspace.

Using a warm washcloth dipped in vinegar, wipe each rim and screw bands. Place lids and rings on each jar and hand tighten.

Place jars in water bather and cover with 1" of water. Process the jars for 10 minutes. Remember, processing time doesn't begin until the water is at a full rolling boil.

Tip!

If you run out of brine, make a half batch of brine, boil and fill jars accordingly. Never fill your remaining jars with just water – it will lessen the acidic level and cause food to spoil.

The Best Bloody Mary

Makes 4 servings

Over the years I have fine-tuned my Bloody Mary making skills by incorporating my home canned goods. Here is what many have said is "The Best Bloody Mary they've ever had."

Ingredients

- 8 strips bacon
- Black pepper
- Steak sauce – I prefer A.1.® steak sauce
- Pickled garlic cloves
- Pickled Brussels sprouts
- Dilly beans
- Pickled asparagus spears
- Pickled serrano peppers
- Dilled baby carrots
- Dill pickles
- 4 stalks of celery
- Your favorite vodka – I prefer Tito's Handmade Vodka®
- 32 ounces of your favorite Bloody Mary Mix – I prefer Zing Zang®
- Celery salt

Instructions

Fry up the bacon until it is just about crisp. Set aside in paper towel to remove grease.

Place 1 teaspoon of steak sauce in each pilsner glass. Using 4 strips of bacon, tear one strip into pieces per pilsner glass covering the steak sauce. Dash twice with black pepper. Add two Pickled Garlic Cloves then fill glass with ice. Add your pickled condiments, celery and remaining bacon to each glass.

Add 2 ounces of vodka to each glass, then add Bloody Mary Mix. Add a dash of celery salt and black pepper to the top and serve.

Raw Sauerkraut

Makes approx. 8 pints or 4 quarts

This fast, simple recipe uses cold storage method to allow fermentation and preservation of sauerkraut. This delicious kraut can be used in any dish where sauerkraut is served whether as a meal or a topping.

Ingredients

16 cups cabbage, shredded

2 teaspoon cumin seeds or 2 teaspoons caraway seeds

2 teaspoons mustard seeds per jar

3 ½ Tablespoons sea salt

5 cups water

4 wide-mouth quart jars

Instructions

In a bowl, mix cabbage with cumin and mustard seeds. Using a potato masher or wooden kitchen mallet, pound/mash the cabbage and seeds for several minutes to release the juices from the cabbage. Fill each quart by tightly packing the cabbage using the opposite end of a wooden spoon or an air bubble remover tool. Give each jar a generous 1" headspace.

Mix water and salt until salt has dissolved. Pour liquid mixture over the cabbage. Using the air bubble remover tool, press the cabbage downward to remove excess air bubbles. Add additional liquid mixture if necessary being sure to keep the generous 1" headspace. Wipe rim of jar with a warm washcloth dipped in vinegar. Add sterilized lids and rings and hand tighten.

Place jars on a dish towel on your countertop in your kitchen and keep at room temperature for 3 days (72 hours) to allow natural fermentation to take place. After 72 hours has passed, transfer to cold storage.

Tip!

Because the jar contents are active during the fermentation process, please note there may be some seepage from the jar prior to and during cold storage. Simply wipe the jars and the surface in which they sit if this occurs. Keep lid and ring secure when wiping.

Ball

Pork Chops with Sauerkraut Dinner

Makes approx. 6 servings

As fall approaches, there is nothing better than utilizing your Raw Sauerkraut in a delicious slow-cooked meal. Serve this dish with a side salad; or place atop mashed potatoes or buttered egg noodles.

Ingredients

2 quarts raw sauerkraut

6 boneless pork chops

1 pound bacon

2 cups chicken stock

1 medium Vidalia onion

5 scallions

8 cloves of garlic, chopped fine

2 Tablespoons extra virgin olive oil

1 Tablespoon freshly chopped parsley, or ½ Tablespoon dried parsley flakes

2 Tablespoons caraway seeds

Sea salt and fresh ground pepper to taste

Instructions

In a medium-sized cast iron skillet, add one Tablespoon of the olive oil and the boneless pork chops. On high heat, brown each side of the chops. Set aside.

Cut your large onion in half then slice into long strips. Slice scallions into long strips as well.

Using the same skillet the chops were browned in, combine remaining olive oil, onions, scallions and chopped garlic. Over medium heat, sauté the mixture until the flavors have blended well and the onions become translucent, about 5 minutes.

Empty your two quarts of raw sauerkraut into a colander over the sink and rinse thoroughly while stirring the kraut. Shake off any excess water and empty kraut into the skillet with the onions. Add parsley, caraway seeds and salt and pepper to taste. Mix well. Add chicken stock, cover and simmer for 15 minutes.

Remove lid and stir well. Add the pork chops to the skillet, cover and resume cooking on low heat for another 15-20 minutes or until kraut and chops are caramelized brown and meat is cooked through.

Tex-Mex Corn Relish

Makes approx. 5 to 6 pints

I love this relish in the summer on bratwursts, and it is scrumptious atop a juicy burger fresh off the grill! It is also a delicious breakfast condiment when served with bacon and eggs! Before you know it, you'll be replacing traditional pickle relish with Tex-Mex Corn Relish.

Ingredients

4 cups white vinegar
1 ½ cups raw sugar
2 Tablespoons sea salt
8 cups whole corn kernels
2 cups green bell pepper
2 cups red bell pepper
1 ½ cups celery, diced
1 cup sweet onion, finely chopped
2 Tablespoons dry mustard
2 teaspoons celery seeds
3 teaspoons ground turmeric
¼ cup water
3 Tablespoons Canning Gel

Instructions

Corn Prep: If using fresh ears of corn, blanch the corn for 3 minutes first before removing kernels. If you are using frozen corn kernels, be sure to thaw and drain the kernels prior to making this recipe.

In a medium-sized stockpot, combine vinegar, sugar and salt. Bring to a boil over medium heat being sure to stir until all sugar is dissolved. Gradually add corn kernels, peppers, celery and onion being sure to keep everything boiling. Stir often to avoid scorching. Add the spices and stir.

In a small bowl, whisk together water and Canning Gel. Stir into the corn mixture while it is boiling. Reduce heat to simmer and boil gently for 5 minutes, stirring often to avoid scorching.

Ladle hot relish into hot jars being sure to leave ½" headspace. Wipe rims with a warm washcloth dipped in vinegar and secure lids and rings. Hand tighten.

Place jars in water bather and cover with 1" of water. Process pints in a hot water bath for 15 minutes. Remember, timing doesn't begin until water is at a full rolling boil.

Tex-Mex Egg Salad Sandwich

Dress up a regular egg salad sandwich with a bit of colorful and flavorful home canned Tex-Mex Corn Relish. Perfect alongside scrambled eggs and scrumptious atop a hardy bratwurst. You'll never use plain 'ol pickle relish again.

Ingredients

4 eggs

½ cup real mayonnaise

1 Tablespoon mustard

½ cup Tex-Mex Corn Relish

4 slices of your favorite bread

Instructions

Cover the eggs with water in a medium-sized pot and bring to a hard boil over high heat. Set timer for 10 minutes. When timer goes off, immediately remove from stove and empty boiling water in sink. Rinse eggs under cool water for 2 minutes, then let sit to cool.

In a mixing bowl, combine mayonnaise, mustard and relish. Mix well.

Once eggs are cool to the touch, crack twice onto a cutting board then gently roll the egg under your palm onto the cutting board surface, gently applying pressure. The shell of the egg will begin to slip off. Remove shells.

Over the mayonnaise mixture, cut hardboiled egg into bits, and mix well. Spread egg salad onto two slices of bread and serve.

CHAPTER 6

Meals in a Jar

With today's busy lifestyle, having a ready-made meal is essential to eating healthy while on the go. Learn how to home can a variety of recipes you simply heat and eat throughout the year.

Chicken Pot Pie Filling

Makes approx. 4 quarts or 8 pints

Having my mom's delicious Chicken Pot Pie Filling on your pantry shelf aides in speedy, healthy meal preparation.

Ingredients

12 large chicken breasts
5 cups carrots, chopped
4 cups frozen peas
2 cups celery, chopped
2 cups onions, chopped
2 cups corn kernels (optional)
4 Tablespoons butter
1 1/3 cups Canning Gel
1 Tablespoon salt
2 teaspoons black pepper
2 teaspoons celery seeds
2 teaspoons garlic powder
8 cups chicken broth

Instructions

Boil chicken breasts in water until cooked through. Measure 8 cups of broth created from boiling the chicken and set aside. If using store bought chicken broth, please be sure to keep 2 cups of cooked broth on hand. Remove cooked chicken from boiled water and set on a cutting board to cool. Once chicken has cooled, chop or tear into bite-sized pieces.

In a large, thick-bottomed stainless steel stockpot combine celery, onions and butter. Sauté on medium heat until onions are translucent, about 8 minutes. Add carrots, peas, corn, chicken, salt, pepper and broth to the onion mixture. Bring to a boil, stirring well. Once at a boil, stir in Canning Gel. Boil for 5 additional minutes then remove from heat.

Ladle hot pie filling into hot jars being sure to leave a generous 1" headspace. Use your air bubble remover tool to remove air pockets and adjust headspace as necessary. Wipe each jar rim and screw band with a warm washcloth dipped in vinegar. Place sterilized lids and rings atop each jar and hand tighten.

Process jars in a pressure canner at 10 pounds of pressure; 75 minutes for pints and 90 minutes for quarts.

Open-faced Chicken & Biscuts

Makes approx. 4 servings

Sometimes ultra-simplistic is the most superb way to enjoy your home canned goods. With a little heat, limited prep and fresh, hot biscuits, your Chicken Pot Pie Filling makes an excellent, quick meal. Needless to say, I keep a ready supply of bake-and-serve biscuits and half-and-half in my refrigerator.

Ingredients

1 quart Chicken Pot Pie Filling

½ cup half-and-half

Salt and pepper to taste

8 biscuits

Instructions

Bake biscuits according to manufacturer's specifications.

While biscuits are in the oven, using a deep saucepan, bring pie filling and half-and-half to a boil over medium-high heat. Add salt and pepper to taste if using. Boil gently for 5 minutes then remove from heat to thicken.

When biscuits are done, remove from oven and open two biscuits on each plate. Spoon hot Chicken Pot Pie Filling atop biscuits and serve.

Tip!

Don't have half-and-half on hand? No worries. Use whole or evaporated milk. You may also round out this meal with a fresh salad or side of warm home canned beets.

Mini Chicken Pot Pies

Makes approx. 4 servings

This dish is a fun change-up from making a large traditional chicken pot pie. Turn your scrumptious filling into adorable, personal pot pies.

Ingredients

1 quart Chicken Pot Pie filling

1 batch of Mumma Newton's Pie Dough

½ cup half-and-half

2 ounces real butter

4 ramekins

Instructions

Preheat oven to 425°F. Grease each ramekin with butter to keep the pie filling from sticking. Set aside.

In a deep saucepan, bring Chicken Pot Pie Filling and half-and-half to boil over medium-high heat. Reduce heat and stir for 1 minute to thicken. Fill each ramekin with hot pie filling.

Roll out dough to ¼" thick. Using a clean ramekin or coffee mug, cut round shapes into the dough. Outline with a knife to ensure a clean cut.

Place dough atop each ramekin, lightly tucking in the sides. Slit the top of the dough in four areas with knife to allow some heat to escape.

Bake for 15-20 minutes or until dough is golden brown and filling is bubbling. Serve hot straight from the ramekin.

Tip!

Don't have time to make my Mumma's dough? No worries. Use store-bought refrigerated dough.

Beef Bourguignon

(aka Beef Burgundy) Makes approx. 6 to 8 quarts

Delicacy in a jar! Once considered a peasant dish, over time it has become a standard in French cuisine. Oh, and did I mention it tastes absolutely delicious? Julia Child described the dish as "certainly one of the most delicious beef dishes concocted by man."

Ingredients

6 pounds chuck roast

6 medium onions, diced large

18 shallots, cut long

12 slices of bacon

5 cups of carrots, peeled and cut in strips

1 Tablespoon sea salt

1 ½ teaspoons black pepper

5 garlic cloves, chopped

3 pounds mushrooms

2 bottles of burgundy wine

1 cup cognac

½ cup extra virgin olive oil

Instructions

Trim your roast by removing excess fat and any silver skin. Keep marbleized fat. Cut into 2 inch strips or chucks. Essentially, cut the beef into the size you prefer to see on the end of your fork.

Pat beef dry with a paper towel so beef will brown properly. In a large skillet, quickly brown beef in batches using a Tablespoon of olive oil at a time. Brown all sides but be careful not to cook the beef. Move quickly – you do not want to cook the beef. After browned, set inside a large stockpot.

Cut bacon into 2 inch pieces. In the skillet using all the beef renderings add the bacon, garlic and olive oil. Cook over medium heat until bacon is done but not crisp. Add diced onions, shallots, mushrooms, salt and pepper and sauté until onions are translucent. Place into the large stockpot with the browned beef. Be sure to scrape every dripping from the skillet into the pot. Mix well.

Add both bottles of wine and the cognac. Bring mixture to a boil on medium heat, stirring often. Once brought to a boil, reduce heat and simmer on low for one hour being sure to stir often to avoid scorching. The goal now is to reduce the wine and blend the flavors. Add carrots and simmer for another hour. Be sure to taste test and add additional salt and pepper to taste, if needed.

Fill hot jars leaving a generous 1" headspace. Remove air bubbles and adjust headspace as necessary. Wipe jar rim with a warm washcloth dipped in vinegar then apply lid and ring. Process in a pressure canner at 10 pounds of pressure; 75 minutes for pints and 90 minutes for quarts.

Beef Burgundy over Garlic Mashed Potatoes

Makes approx. 4 servings

Turn your delicacy in a jar into a robust meal using homemade garlic mashed potatoes. If time is of the essence, you may make the garlic mashed potatoes ahead of time and freeze for up to one month prior to thawing, heating and enjoying.

Ingredients

2 quarts Beef Burgundy

8 russet potatoes, peeled and halved

1 head of garlic

1 Tablespoon extra-virgin olive oil

¼ cup real butter

½ cup milk

½ cup Romano or Parmesan cheese

1 teaspoon sea salt

½ teaspoon black pepper

Instructions

Preheat oven to 425°F.

Cut off the top of the head of garlic, about the first half-inch, to expose the majority of the cloves without cutting the cloves in half. Place the garlic head inside a ramekin and drizzle with oil. Place in oven on the top shelf to roast.

In a stockpot, cover potatoes with water. Add a pinch of salt and bring to a hard boil. Boil for about 20 minutes or until potatoes are soft.

In a deep saucepan, bring Beef Burgundy to a gentle boil over medium-high heat. Stir often.

Drain potatoes and place in large, clean mixing bowl. Using a fork or hand masher, crush each potato into small chunks. Remove the garlic head from the oven. Using heat-proof gloves, squeeze the base of the head above the mixing bowl. The softened garlic cloves should slip right out. Puncture skin with a paring knife to remove any remaining cloves and empty into mixing bowl. Mash the garlic cloves into the potatoes.

Add remaining ingredients to mixing bowl. Either by hand or using a hand beater, beat ingredients together until desired consistency is reached, using a spatula to scrape mixture off sides of the bowl.

Plate the mashed potatoes, spoon hot Beef Burgundy atop potatoes and serve.

Chili con Carne

Makes approx. 9 to 12 quarts

No matter the season, it is sheer delight having a quart of this hearty meal sitting on your pantry shelf. Entertaining guests? Cut out the interior of a round loaf of bread making an edible bread bowl.

To the Jar

Ingredients

5 pounds of hamburger

2 pounds Italian sausage

12 cups Roma tomatoes, chopped

2 bell peppers, finely chopped

2 cups onions, finely chopped

5-8 garlic cloves, minced

1 jalapeño, deseeded and finely chopped

4 large stalks, parsley – finely chopped

1 cup chili powder

¼ cup cumin powder

1 teaspoon cumin seeds

1-2 teaspoons red pepper flakes

6-8 drops Tabasco® sauce

4 teaspoons course canning salt

Black pepper to taste

½ pound dried black beans

½ pound dried kidney beans

¼ pound dried pinto beans

Instructions

The acid from the tomatoes will prevent the beans from softening, so we must rehydrate dried beans prior to adding to chili base. Rinse and sort beans in a large colander. Place dried beans in a large stockpot and cover beans entirely with water. Bring to a boil. Boil hard for 2 minutes, stirring often, then remove from heat. Cover and let soak for 1 hour.

Brown meat and sausage in a large, thick-bottomed stainless steel stockpot. Remove excess grease. Set aside.

Add everything but tomatoes and beans to meat mixture. Stir well and cook on medium-heat until onions are translucent and tender, about 5 minutes.

Drain beans in colander. Add tomatoes and beans to the stockpot. Mix well. Bring contents to a boil on medium-high heat, stirring often to avoid scorching. Reduce heat and boil gently for 10-15 minutes, stirring often.

Ladle chili into hot quart-sized jars being sure to leave a generous 1" headspace. Wipe the jar rims and screw bands with a warm washcloth dipped in vinegar. Place lids and rings on each jar and hand tighten. Pressure can at 10 pounds of pressure; 90 minutes for quarts and 75 minutes for pints.

Chili con Carne Omelet

A hearty breakfast is the perfect way to start your day – and nothing says hearty like chili con carne. Turn a simplistic omelet into an amazing meal.

To the Table

Ingredients

1 Tablespoon butter

2 eggs

1 Tablespoon milk

Salt and pepper to taste

1 Tablespoon fresh chives, chopped

¼ cup shredded cheddar cheese

1 pint Chili con Carne

Sour cream

Instructions

Crack eggs into a small mixing bowl. Beat eggs with a fork. Add milk, salt, pepper, shredded cheese and half the chives. Mix well and set aside.

Heat an 8-inch omelet pan over high heat. Add butter and tilt pan to ensure butter thoroughly coats the bottom of the pan. With fork, mix eggs well and pour directly into the center of the pan, tilting again so the egg mixture coats bottom of the pan. Using a spatula, gently move cheese evenly throughout the eggs. Turn burner down to medium heat.

Allow egg mixture to cook and firm, about 3 minutes. Cook until the egg mixture begins to hold together and the center is no longer runny. Add 3 Tablespoons of chili con carne to the center, spreading out toward one side of the circle, keeping the chili ¼" away from the edge.

Using your spatula and gently tilting the pan, flip the non-chili side of the omelet atop the chili side. In a fluid motion, gently lift the pan and slide the omelet onto your serving plate using the spatula. Adjust shape as needed. Garnish the top of your omelet with a dollop of sour cream and a sprinkle of the remaining chives. Serve hot.

Mom's Homemade Chicken Soup

Makes approx. 8 quarts or 16 pints

A staple in my pantry and especially handy during the cold and flu season, I consider this family recipe Nature's Penicillin! Add noodles or rice when reheating a jar for a fun, filling meal.

Ingredients

8 quarts of water

1 whole chicken, including carcass and skin

3 bay leaves

5 garlic cloves, chopped fine

1 Tablespoon crushed basil

1 Tablespoon sea salt

2 teaspoons black pepper

2 cups onion, diced

6 cups carrots, chopped

2 cups celery, chopped

2 cups Idaho potatoes, diced

1 pint Basil Diced Tomatoes (Page 89)

Instructions

Place water, chicken and bay leaves in a large stockpot and bring to boil. Reduce heat to medium and boil chicken until cooked through, approximately 30 minutes. Be sure to stir chicken often to avoid scorching from resting at the bottom of the stockpot. Once cooked through, remove chicken and set aside on cutting board to cool to touch. Keep water as this is the soup base.

Remove all skin and bones from chicken. Using either a knife or your fingers, cut/tear chicken into bite-size pieces until all meat (both light and dark) have been removed from the carcass. Add chicken and remaining ingredients back to stockpot and bring to a boil. Boil for 5 minutes ,stirring often.

Hot pack soup into prepared jars being sure to leave a 1" headspace. Feel free to hot pack any remaining liquid to process and use later as chicken stock. Wipe each rim with a warm washcloth dipped in vinegar. Place lid and rings on each jar and hand tighten. Pressure quarts at 10 pounds of pressure; 90 minutes for quarts and 75 minutes for pints.

Tip!

So your food to liquid ratio is suitable when reheating and eating, use a slotted spoon and fill jars ¾ the way full with solids prior to ladling broth into the jar. This will help avoid having too much, or too little broth in your bowl while enjoying your soup for dinner.

Chicken Tortilla Soup

Makes approx. 8 quarts or 16 pints

This authentic flavored soup has amazing body and boasts delicious flavor! Prior to serving, top each bowl with thin tortilla strips, shredded cheese, a dollop of sour cream and dash of hot sauce.

Ingredients

4 large boneless, skinless chicken breasts

1 ½ cups carrots, sliced half-moon shaped ½" thick

1 large Vidalia onion, diced

16 Roma tomatoes, diced

2 cups dried black beans

1 cup mild green chilies, chopped fine

2 cups water

6 cups chicken stock

4 cups corn kernels

1 Tablespoon ground cumin

1 Tablespoon sea salt

1 Tablespoon ground chili powder

1 teaspoon paprika

1 teaspoon oregano

2-4 dried cayenne peppers

6 garlic cloves, minced

2 Tablespoons Canning Gel

Instructions

In a small stockpot, cover chicken breasts with 2" of water and boil until cooked through, about 15 minutes. Remove chicken and set aside to cool. Discard water. Once chicken has cooled, shred or cut into bite size pieces.

Dried black beans may be added to the soup once they have been properly cleaned and rinsed in a colander. The beans will soften naturally during processing.

In a large stockpot, combine all ingredients and bring to a boil on medium-high heat, mixing well. Reduce heat and simmer for 5 minutes. Remove dried cayenne peppers from soup and discard.

Using a slotted spoon and funnel, fill your hot jars ¾ full with soup contents. Next, ladle soup broth being sure to leave a generous 1" headspace. Remove any air bubbles and adjust headspace as necessary.

Using a warm washcloth dipped in vinegar, wipe jar rim and screw bands. Place sterilized lid and ring atop each jar and hand tighten. Pressure quarts at 10 pounds of pressure; 90 minutes for quarts and 75 minutes for pints.

Spaghetti Sauces

These are my go-to jars when making a variety of meals that require a red sauce base. There are three different varieties – traditional, zesty and a meatless garden blend. Each variety exemplifies three different flavors. The benefit of having three different sauces is you never tire of using red sauce giving you the option to choose which variety best suites your mood, your palette and the meal being created.

For me, spaghetti sauce is often times the best choice given my family's busy work, school and sports schedule. Straight out of the jar, each is fantastic over any type of noodle. Each of my spaghetti sauces will give you a quick, healthy meal choice to avoid hitting up the drive-thru for fast food.

Zesty Spaghetti Sauce

Makes approx. 14 pints or 7 quarts

Ingredients

- 30 pounds Roma tomatoes, approx. a half-bushel
- 14 dried California chili peppers
- 1 ½ pounds ground beef
- 1 ½ pounds Italian sausage
- 1 ½ cups onions, chopped
- 1 cup green pepper, seeded and chopped
- 5 Tablespoons garlic, minced
- 6 Tablespoons fresh parsley, coarsely chopped
- 4 Tablespoons fresh basil
- ½ cup packed brown sugar
- 2 Tablespoons dried oregano
- 4 teaspoons sea salt
- 3 teaspoons black pepper

Traditional Spaghetti Sauce

Makes approx. 14 pints or 7 quarts

Ingredients

30 pounds Roma tomatoes, approx. a half-bushel

1 ½ pounds ground beef

1 ½ pounds Italian sausage

1 ½ cups onions, chopped

1 cup green pepper, seeded and chopped

½ pound mushrooms, sliced (optional)

5 Tablespoons garlic, minced

6 Tablespoons fresh parsley, coarsely chopped

4 Tablespoons fresh basil

½ cup packed brown sugar

2 Tablespoons dried oregano

4 teaspoons sea salt

3 teaspoons black pepper

Garden Spaghetti Sauce

Makes approx. 14 pints or 7 quarts

Ingredients

30 pounds Roma tomatoes, approx. a half-bushel

3 cups carrots, finely chopped

3 cups zucchini, shredded

1 cup summer squash, shredded

1 celery stalk, finely chopped

1 ½ cups onions, chopped

1 cup green pepper, seeded and chopped

½ pound mushrooms, sliced (optional)

5 Tablespoons garlic, minced

6 Tablespoons fresh parsley, coarsely chopped

4 Tablespoons fresh basil

½ cup packed brown sugar

2 Tablespoons dried oregano

4 teaspoons sea salt

3 teaspoons black pepper

Instructions

Tomato Prep: Core and cut tomatoes into quarters and purée in a food processor. Place purée in a large, thick-bottomed stainless steel stockpot. Bring to a boil over medium-high heat, stirring frequently to avoid scorching. Once to a boil, reduce heat and boil gently for 10 minutes. Remove from heat and set aside.

Chili Purée (for Zesty Spaghetti Sauce): Remove stems and place in a stainless steel bowl. Cover peppers with boiling water and submerge dried peppers for 20 minutes. To fully submerge the peppers, use a salad plate atop the peppers and rest a soup bowl full of hot water on top of the plate.

Once rehydrated, place reconstituted chilies and a ½ cup of liquid into your food processor and purée. Set aside.

Meat/Spices (for Traditional & Zesty Spaghetti Sauce): In a skillet, cook sausage and hamburger until done. Drain any excess fat. Add onions, green peppers, garlic, mushrooms, parsley, basil, oregano, salt and black pepper. Cook on medium heat until onions are clear and peppers are soft.

Vegetables/Spices (for Garden Spaghetti Sauce): In a skillet, add onions, green peppers, garlic, mushrooms, parsley, basil, oregano, salt and black pepper. Cook on medium heat until onions are clear and peppers are soft. Add remaining vegetables, mix well, and cook for 5 minutes to blend flavors.

Add the meat, vegetable or chili purée to the tomatoes. Stir in brown sugar. Bring to a boil over medium-high heat, stirring often. Boil gently for 5 minutes. Hot pack sauce into jars leaving 1" of headspace. Wipe jar rims and screw bands with a washcloth dipped in vinegar and secure sterilized lids and rings. Hand tighten. Pressure cook at 10 pounds of pressure; quarts for 70 minutes and pints for 60 minutes.

Tip!

I have learned it takes approximately 18 average-sized Roma tomatoes to equal 8 cups of food-processed tomatoes. Also, the skin of a Roma tomato is very thin and can be used in canning recipes without blanching. Traditional canning tomatoes should be blanched and the skins removed when used to make sauce.

Spaghetti with Meatballs

Makes approx. 4 servings

A juicy meatball packed with tons of flavor. The perfect addition to Garden, Traditional and Zesty spaghetti sauce.

Ingredients

1 pound lean ground beef

½ pound Italian sausage

2 eggs, beaten

¼ cup milk

3 slices Italian bread, ripped into tiny pieces

½ cup grated Romano cheese

1 small onion, finely chopped

3 garlic cloves, minced

2 Tablespoons of fresh or dehydrated parsley

1 Tablespoon Worcestershire sauce

¼ teaspoon black pepper

2 Tablespoons extra-virgin olive oil

1 quart spaghetti sauce

1 half-pint tomato paste

Instructions

In a saucepan, heat spaghetti sauce on medium. Stir in tomato paste, simmer to thicken. Stir often.

While sauce is thickening, crack eggs into a large bowl and beat well. Add milk and beat. Add bread, onions, garlic, parsley, Worcestershire sauce and parsley. Mix well.

Using your hands, crumble the hamburger and sausage into the egg mixture. Add grated Romano cheese atop meat. Mix and squeeze ingredients with both hands, blending and mixing everything well.

Shape meat into 2" balls, rolling each in the palm of your hands. Add oil to skillet and heat on medium. Add meatballs into the skillet being careful not to splatter the oil. Pan fry on each side for about 15 minutes total or until cooked through. Be sure to continue to check your sauce and stir.

Drain grease and place each meatball into the sauce. Stir gently, coating each meatball with sauce. Cook for an additional 5 minutes. Serve hot atop your favorite pasta.

Stuffed Shells

Makes approx. 8 to 10 servings

This is a very popular recipe in my home – and perfect when entertaining guests. Authentic Italian ingredients beautifully highlight your home canned spaghetti sauce.

Ingredients

25-30 jumbo pasta shells

1 pound Italian sausage

1 medium onion, finely chopped

6-8 white button mushrooms, finely chopped

15 ounces Ricotta cheese

4 garlic cloves, minced

1 large egg, beaten

1 teaspoon sea salt

½ teaspoon black pepper

2 cups grated Romano cheese

1 cup Mozzarella cheese

1 cup spinach leaves

1 quart Garden, Traditional or Zesty Spaghetti sauce

Instructions

Preheat oven to 375° F. Bring a large stockpot of lightly salted water to boil. Add shells one at a time to avoid shells nesting. Return to a boil, then cover and remove from heat. Let stand 10 minutes then drain and rinse with hot water. Set aside.

Cook sausage in a skillet for 5 minutes, breaking apart any clumps. Add onions, garlic and mushrooms and cook until onions are translucent. Add spinach and cook until wilted. Remove from heat to cool.

In a large mixing bowl, combine Ricotta cheese, egg, salt and pepper, 1 cup Romano and ½ cup Mozzarella cheese. Mix well. Add the cooled sausage mixture and mix well. Set aside.

In a medium-sized pot, warm spaghetti sauce through on medium-high heat. Using a 9x13 glass baking dish, spread 1 cup spaghetti sauce across the bottom of the dish.

Fill each shell with the sausage mixture, about 3 to 4 Tablespoons per shell, and set in glass baking dish. After dish is filled with stuffed shells, dabble a spoonful of spaghetti sauce atop each stuffed shell.

Cover with foil and bake for 25 minutes, or until sauce is bubbling. Remove foil and sprinkle the remaining cheeses overtop. Return to oven uncovered for 8 to 10 minutes, or until cheese is melted. Serve with additional spaghetti sauce and a side salad.

Beef Stew with Vegetables

Makes approx. 7 quarts

This hearty meal is sure to please. Filled with a variety of vegetables, herbs and beautiful cuts of meat. It is best enjoyed alongside freshly baked bread.

Ingredients

2 Tablespoons extra virgin olive oil

5 pounds of stewing beef, cut in 1 ½" cubes

12 cups potatoes, peeled and cubed

8 cups carrots, peeled and chopped

3 cups celery, chopped

3 cups onions, chopped

1 pint jar Basil Diced Tomatoes (page 89) or 5 Roma tomatoes, diced

1 Tablespoon parsley flakes

1 Tablespoon dried oregano

½ Tablespoon celery seed

1 teaspoon ground coriander

1 teaspoon dried thyme

1 teaspoon dried basil

½ teaspoons ground black pepper

4 ½ teaspoons sea salt

2 quarts home canned beef broth

5 cups boiling water

2 beef bouillon cubes (optional)

Instructions

In a large skillet, starting with one Tablespoon of oil olive, brown beef in batches. Be sure not to cook the meat, just simply brown each side of the meat cube and remove from skillet. Transfer browned beef – and the drippings from the skillet – into a large, thick-bottomed stainless steel stockpot. Add all prepared vegetables and seasonings to the meat. Mix well.

Add beef broth. Add 4 cups of boiling water to the mix. If using beef bouillon cubes, add now. If needed, add additional boiling water to just cover the meat and vegetable mixture.

Bring the contents of the stockpot to a boil using medium-high heat being sure to stir frequently. Allow to boil for 5 minutes, then remove from heat. Ladle beef stew into hot jars, leaving a 1" headspace. Remove any air bubbles and adjust headspace as necessary. Wipe rim and screw bands with a warm washcloth dipped in vinegar, then add lids and rings. Hand tighten.

Process in a pressure canner at 10 pounds of pressure; 75 minutes for pints and 90 minutes for quarts.

Tip!

When heating a quart of stew for dinner, feel free to thicken the stew with 3 Tablespoons of Canning Gel on the stove top and serve over garlic mashed potatoes. Divine!

Beef Tips & Gravy with Whole Garlic Cloves

Makes approx. 6 to 8 pints

Having jars of this protein-packed meat on the ready will make excellent meal starters! Reheat this seasoned, cooked meat and serve alongside vegetables, atop mashed potatoes or mix with cooked egg noodles for a quick meal. You may also use these scrumptious bits when making soups and stews.

Ingredients

10-12 pounds stew beef

8-16 garlic whole cloves

2-4 Tablespoons of extra virgin olive oil

2 teaspoons sea salt

1 teaspoons black pepper, ground

½ cup Canning Gel

4 cups hot water

Instructions

Meat Prep: Choose the highest cut of meat you prefer to eat. Trim away gristle, remove excess fat and silver skin and any bruising. Cut meat into 1"-2" thick chunks, cubes or strips, or purchase pre-cut stew meat from the butcher.

Pat your meat dry with paper towel so it will brown properly. In a deep skillet, sear the meat in batches using 1 Tablespoon of olive oil at a time. Dash each batch with sea salt and black pepper. Work quickly, searing on all sides. Do not to cook the meat! It is literally in the pan for seconds on each side. Set aside. Leave the delicious drippings in the skillet.

Add 4 cups of hot water to skillet. Whisk in Canning Gel and bring liquid mixture to a quick boil, stirring frequently. Boil for 2 minutes then remove from heat. Set gravy aside.

Add 1-2 whole garlic cloves to each warm jar. Pack meat, leaving a generous 1" headspace. Ladle hot gravy mixture over top of meat being sure to keep the generous 1" headspace. Remove air bubbles using your bubble remover tool and add more gravy as necessary.

Wipe jar rims with a warm washcloth dipped in vinegar and add lids and rings. Hand tighten. Process jars at 10 pounds of pressure; pints for 75 minutes and quarts for 90 minutes.

Beef Tips with Carrots over Noodles

Makes approx. 4 servings

There are many advantages to having ready-made meals on hand. Sometimes reheating a combination of several home canned goods is all it takes to have a quick, healthy meal in minutes. This dinner is a popular one in my home.

Ingredients

1 quart Beef Tips & Gravy with Whole Garlic Cloves

1 pint home canned carrots, drained

Fresh cracked black pepper

8-10 ounces egg noodles

Fresh black pepper

Canning Gel

Instructions

Cook egg noodles until tender, drain and set aside. Empty Beef Tips & Gravy into a deep saucepan and heat on medium high for 5 minutes.

Drain carrots and add to saucepan. Mix well without breaking apart carrots. Bring to a boil and simmer for 2 minutes.

Give the egg noodles a quick rinse in hot water if they begin to stick together. Shake off excess water and add to meat mixture. Mix well being sure everything is coated with gravy.

Heat for an additional 2 minutes. Plate hot. Crack two turns of fresh cracked black pepper. Serve hot.

Tip!

If you prefer more gravy, mix 1 heaping Tablespoon of Canning Gel with 1 cup of hot water. Then stir liquid into meat mixture prior to carrots and noodles. Bring to a boil and simmer as specified in the recipe.

Canned Chicken Breasts

Makes approx. 7 quarts or 17 pints

Having canned chicken on hand is a real time-saver! Simply reheat using a stove top, and create meals like Chicken Quesadillas, Chicken Curry Soup, Chicken Tacos, Enchiladas and Chicken Alfredo. Home canned chicken is even great to take camping. The possibilities are endless!

Ingredients

Approx. 25-30 whole boneless chicken breasts

Water

Instructions

Remove excess fat from meat. Cut breasts into usable pieces (about 2" in size). Each quart will fit approximately 3 ½ chicken breasts. Raw pack each quart, leaving a generous 1" headspace.

Add water being sure to keep the generous 1" headspace. Using your headspace/air bubble remover tool, remove all air bubbles and adjust water level accordingly. Chicken will lay atop each piece in the jar; use the tool to move the meat to ensure water encircles the meat fully and bubbles are removed.

Wipe rim and screw bands with warm washcloth dipped in vinegar. Apply lids and rings and hand tighten. Pressure can chicken at 10-12 pounds of pressure; 90 minutes for quarts and 75 minutes for pints.

Tip!

Prefer dark meat? No worries. You may can thighs following the recipe above. Drumsticks — leave the bone in and reduce processing time to 75 minutes for quarts and 65 minutes for pints.

Homemade Dried Spice Blends

Adding dried herbs and spices to your home canned goods gives you a leg up during meal preparation. There are a variety of dishes I create with my home canned chicken, so permeating the meat during pressure canning gives my meals added flavor. These are also great blends for canning tomatoes.

Ingredients

Taco/Chili Seasoning Spice Blend

2 Tablespoons chili powder

2 teaspoons garlic powder

2 teaspoons onion powder

2 teaspoons crushed red pepper flakes

2 teaspoons dried oregano

2 teaspoons paprika

2 teaspoons ground cumin

2 teaspoons ground coriander

1 ½ teaspoons sea salt

1 teaspoons black pepper

Italian Spice Blend

4 teaspoons dried Basil

2 teaspoons dried Thyme

3 teaspoons dried Oregano

2 teaspoons dried Rosemary

1 teaspoon dried Sage

1 ½ teaspoons garlic powder

½ teaspoon hot pepper flakes (optional)

Asian Spice Blend

2 Tablespoons yellow curry powder

2 teaspoons garlic powder

2 teaspoons onion powder

2 teaspoons gingerroot powder

1 ½ sea salt

1 tsp black pepper

Instructions

Mix well and store in half-pint jars out of direct sunlight. Label lids.

When canning chicken or tomatoes, add 2 ½ teaspoons per pint jar or 1 ½ Tablespoons per quart jar.

Pulled Mexican Chicken

Makes approx. 8 servings

Authentic flavors and slow cooked to perfection, this easy and delicious meal is sure to please.

Ingredients

- 3 long sweet red peppers – stemmed, seeded and cut lengthwise then sliced
- 1 large Vidalia onion – trimmed and cut in half then sliced
- 5 garlic cloves – peeled and chopped rough
- 3 quarts Home Canned Chicken
- 4 Tablespoons apple cider vinegar
- 10 Roma tomatoes – diced
- 4 ounces tomato paste
- 4 Tablespoons Agave Sweetener
- 2 Tablespoons mustard
- 1 teaspoon onion powder
- 2 Tablespoons cumin
- 3 Tablespoons chili powder
- 1 Tablespoon dried oregano
- 2 Tablespoons coriander
- 2 teaspoons Tabasco® sauce
- 2 Tablespoons of your favorite hot sauce
- 2 Tablespoons of Grape Seed or Extra Virgin Olive Oil
- Corn tortillas and/or white rice

Instructions

Preheat oven to 425°F. In a glass baking dish, layer the bottom with sweet peppers, onions and garlic.

Open and drain your jars of home canned chicken. Place in a skillet on medium-high, add oil and heat through, then lay atop the bed of peppers and onions.

In the same skillet, add the remaining ingredients and bring to a boil on medium-high heat. Once at a boil, reduce heat and simmer for 5 minutes. Pour mixture atop the chicken being sure to thoroughly cover chicken.

Cover baking dish with foil and cook for 40 minutes. When done, remove from the oven and let rest 5 minutes. Mix well.

In a clean sauté pan, heat corn tortillas for 20 seconds on each side. Fill each warm tortilla with the pulled chicken mixture or serve atop a bed of white rice. Add your favorite toppings like shredded cheese, diced onions or sour cream.